The
LEARNING
Spirit

The
LEARNING
Spirit

Lessons from South Africa

Ana K. Gobledale

Chalice Press
St. Louis, Missouri

Biblical quotations, unless otherwise noted, are from the Holy Bible. New International Version, copyright © 1978 by the New York International Bible Society. Used by permission of Zondervan Bible Publishers.

Those quotations marked TEV are from the *Good News Bible*—Old Testament: Copyright © American Bible Society 1976. New Testament Copyright © American Bible Society 1966, 1971, 1976. Used by permission.

Cover design: Anna Bryant
Art Director: Michael Dominguez

10 9 8 7 6 5 4 3 2 1

Library of Congress Cataloging–in–Publication Data

Gobledale, Ana K.
    The learning spirit : lessons from South Africa / Ana K.
Gobledale.
      p. cm.
    Includes bibliographical references.
    ISBN 0-8272-2124-X
    1. Gobledale, Ana K. 2. Gobledale, Tod. 3. United   Congregational Churches of Southern Africa—Clergy—
Biography. 4. Congregationalist churches—South Africa—
Clergy—Biography. 5. Race relations—Religious aspects—
Christianity. 6. South Africa—Race relations. 7. Christianity
and   justice—South Africa. 8. Kwazula (South Africa)—Social
conditions. 9. Natal (South Africa)—Social   conditions.
10. South Africa—Church history—20th   century. I. Title
BX7260.G54A3 1994   94-32058
285.8'68491—dc20   CIP

Printed in the United States of America

DEDICATION

This book is dedicated to my friend, Nokukhanya Dludla, whose spirit continues to teach and inspire me. Nokukhanya was buried in the hills of Mfanefile, South Africa, in March 1993.

THANKS

To my dear friends and colleagues in the ministry—Art Vaeni, Tobias Paddock, Judith Gooch, and Barbara Earl—for encouraging me to continue to grow in the light of God.

To my kindred spirits—Lindley Kinerk, Susan Andy Jepson, Wendy Garvey, and John Garvey—for living in truth and urging me to trust.

To my beloved husband, Tod, for sharing this journey with me. For seeking truth, for trusting in God and for living creatively in service to others. Thanks, too, for letting me include your stories from South Africa.

To others too numerous to name including those who read, reread, edited, led me through the mires of computer technology, and encouraged me—especially Frank Richards, Michael Mello, Phyllis Cunningham, Glenn Smith, Sherman Stanage, John Ohliger, Parker Palmer, Ted Goble, and the Sulloway Hollis & Soden law firm of Concord, New Hampshire.

FOREWORD

Archbishop Desmond M. Tutu

During some of the darkest moments of apartheid's harassment, I received the newsletter of a Lutheran parish in Alaska. There I learned that we who were in the struggle for justice in South Africa were being prayed for, and the newsletter contained our names. We were being prayed for—by name—halfway around the world in Alaska. How could we not eventually win?

One of the most wonderful things about being harassed and in trouble with your government because of trying to be obedient to Jesus Christ is discovering the exhilarating reality of being a member of the church of God. You have all this family around the globe, most of whom you will not meet this side of death, and they are praying for you, and love you, and uphold you. We are connected to one another in the Spirit. And as we grow closer to God, so are we drawn closer to one another.

Part of the South African government's harassment during those years of apartheid led to its appointing a judicial commission, the Eloff Commission, to investigate the South African Council of Churches. Its purpose was to discredit us, so that none of our overseas friends and partners would want to touch us with the proverbial barge pole. As it happened, the government was hoisted on its own petard. By making a few international telephone calls we had the most impressive array of overseas church leaders and delegations to descend on South Africa in a long time, to testify on behalf of the SACC. That was a tremendous act of solidarity, and the government ended up with considerable egg on its face.

The evil that was apartheid is over now. We thank God for that. And we thank all our dear friends for the love and support of economic sanctions and other forms of pressure, together with fervent prayers, that brought us to this day when a new South Africa is being shaped. You have a substantial share in that victory.

But the consequences of apartheid's evil are still with us. The effects of decades of human degradation and poverty and lack of education and joblessness and family separation and oppressed rage and violence will not disappear overnight. Ana Gobledale's narrative of the South Africa she experienced continues to be relevant for understanding the time that is now being born—and for understanding your own experience as well.

We have received so much from the North and have given hardly anything in return. I want to suggest that Americans consider a small gift we in Africa just might be able to offer. It is the gift of *ubuntu*. That is difficult to translate into English, but *ubuntu* is the essence of being human. It declares that my humanity is caught up and inextricably bound up in yours. I am because I belong. That's one reason why these vignettes of one person's encounter with apartheid now become part of your life also.

The West has made wonderful strides in its impressive technological achievements and material prosperity. But its dominant ethic of achievement and success is taking its toll. People feel worthless, are often considered worthless, if they do not achieve. The worst thing that can happen to anyone is to fail. You must succeed at whatever cost. Profits, things, are often prized above people. *Ubuntu* might remind us of a biblical truth—that all that we are, all that we have, is gift. We are because God loved us, loves us, and will love us forever. And because of that unswerving love, we are free to grow in being more gentle, more caring, more compassionate—more in touch with the God who embraces us unconditionally.

Such a spirituality, such an authentic encounter with God, will invariably send us away to look with the eyes of God, to hear with the ears of God, to feel with the heart of God, what is happening anywhere in God's world. It will open us up to the Learning Spirit.

CONTENTS

Introduction

In 1984, my husband, Tod, and I were called by the United Congregational Church of Southern Africa (UCCSA) to co-pastor a circuit of twenty-five congregations scattered throughout northern Zululand. We chose to live in the rural Zulu community of Mfanefile, where one of these congregations is situated. The Republic of South Africa became our home for almost seven years.

As white middle-class Americans, we faced many adjustments. We chose to break the law of apartheid and lived illegally in an area reserved for black Africans. Living among the most oppressed and victimized population group in South Africa, we found ourselves constantly confronted by the injustice of apartheid.

Tod and I recorded incidents in our life in South Africa that clarified for us the myths[1] of the apartheid system under which we lived. These incidents jolted our perspective and changed our outlook. While some of the events occurred to Tod, the experiences have become shared through the process of reflection and writing. These stories form the heart of this book.

Our experiences are not all-encompassing. They are narrow and limited. My lens is that of a "First World" middle-class white woman, a member of the status quo. My focus is on a series of events, most of which occurred in a small corner of Zululand (now known as KwaZulu-Natal) in the vast Republic of South Africa. I have tried to interact with these experiences and to be educated, to interact with truth as it unfolds around me and to let the light break through and illuminate my experiences. Rather than rely on clichés and government "lines" to understand situations, I have tried to free my thoughts from such limiting "answers" and to discern genuine truth.

In the midst of this process of reflection and clarification, I realized that this was not the first time my life had been interrupted by a transformative event that radically changed my perspective of the world. I recalled moments from earlier years in which a similar jolting of perspective and change of outlook had occurred in me. I began to question when and how this phenomenon of life-changing genuine education occurs. I called these transforming moments, this experience of being open to genuine learning, the "Learning Spirit."

In this book I share my story, offering a window into the depths of one person's experience of transforming moments. I weave together accounts of learning incidents in South Africa, parallel events earlier in my life, and events that have occurred since my return to the United States in December 1991 that reveal my experiences of the Learning Spirit.

As my life has unfolded, I have moved from an experience of intense fear and despair into the experience of enlightenment. I have moved out of a state of spiritual separateness—separated from parts of myself, from other human beings, from the higher power in my life (which I call God),[2] and from my powers of learning and creating. Similar to the blinded Saul under the healing hand of Ananias, I have experienced "something like scales" (Acts 9:18) falling from my eyes. I have moved into an experience of clarity, of understanding, of freedom, of trust. I have moved out of an experience of sin[3] into an experience of grace.

While seeming bold to describe myself as being in the experience of grace, I certainly realize that any intellectual understanding of my enlightenment remains susceptible to forms of self-deception. This possibility can never be completely discounted.[4] There is, I know, a fine line between humility and pride. I perceive that the moment I claim humility, it is a proud claim. Yet being humble, being grateful, and remaining teachable is the attitude for which I strive.

The validity of the truth I uncover as I analyze my experiences lies not in the scientific realm, but in the internal reality of the experiences. I have had internal experiences that provide evidence disputable by those who have not had the experiences, as a deaf person would deny the experience of music. It is not my wish to enter into a dispute with one who lacks this internal experience. Nothing will be gained and the issue at stake will likely be lost.

Thomas Merton writes, "If a writer is so cautious that [one] never writes anything that cannot be criticized, [one] will never write anything that can be read. If you want to help other people you have got to make up your mind to write things that some people will condemn."[5]

And so I write with a threefold goal in mind: to introduce the concept of the Learning Spirit, to reveal the often-hidden horrors of apartheid and the racism that upheld it, and to offer reflections helpful for the person who wishes to name her or his own demons and be free.

"Light has come into the world, but [people] loved darkness instead of light because their deeds were evil. Everyone who does evil hates the light, and will not come into the light for fear that [their] deeds will be exposed. But whoever lives by the truth comes into the light, so that it may be seen plainly that what [they have] done has been done through God."

John 3:19–21

Notes

To facilitate easy reading, I have taken the liberty of making quotations inclusive.

[1] I use the term *myth* in a similar fashion to John F. Kennedy's usage in his statement, "The great enemy of the truth is very often not the lie—deliberate, contrived and dishonest—but the myth, persistent, persuasive and unrealistic." Cited in *For Today* (Torrance, California: Overeaters Anonymous, Inc., 1982), 12.

[2] As the Old Testament prophet Jeremiah so aptly declares, "If I say, 'I will not mention God...,' God's word is in my heart like a burning fire, shut up in my bones. I am weary of holding it in; indeed, I cannot" (Jeremiah 20:9). So it is for me.

[3] I use the term *sin* not in a moralistic sense but rather in the manner of the theologian Paul Tillich: to describe the state of being separated from self, from others, and from our ultimate reality—God.

[4] See Jürgen Habermas, *Toward a Rational Society* (Boston: Beacon Press, 1971), 218-19. Cited in Jack Mezirow, "A Critical Theory in Adult Education." *Adult Education* 32, No. 1 (1981), 8.

[5] Thomas Merton, *New Seeds of Contemplation* (New York: New Directions Publishing Corporation, 1962), 105.

1

ENGAGED BY THE LEARNING SPIRIT

There is only one great thing
The only thing
To live,
To see the great day that dawns,
And the light that fills the world.
—Inuit song

Welcome Home

"*Amandla!*"

"*Awethu!*"

"*Power to the people!*" *The cries carom around the airport arrival hall. The three freed prisoners—Kevin, Allan, and Vincent—raise their hands high as they are engulfed by their friends.*

Kevin, Allan, and Vincent: imprisoned in 1986 and 1987 for "furthering the cause of the African National Congress." The press would have us believe these men are hardened terrorists. But amidst luggage carts and travel posters, the three young men seem ordinary as they are welcomed home. In spite of their years of imprisonment on Robben Island, they appear healthy. From across the arrival hall I view the crowd, mostly middle-class young adults in running shoes and stone-washed designer jeans. They are excited to be reunited with those taken away from their midst, taken by the government in an effort to break resistance to apartheid.

Kevin, Allan, and Vincent: there is nothing remarkable in their appearance. Kevin reminds me of a panda bear in his heavy char-

5

coal overcoat. He carries the guitar that likely kept him company in his cell. A gold cross dangles on his chest. The crowd hoists him to their shoulders. His round face splits with a smile. His eyes twinkle with tears.

I stand in my safe spot beside a stone pillar. I feel like stone myself rooted by my fear, held back by a small internal voice whispering persistently, "Don't get involved. It's not your crowd. Let them do their own thing." I've stood and watched, merely a spectator, waiting for my midnight flight to Johannesburg.

I angrily ponder, "Why aren't there any whites in the welcoming party? Why aren't there any church delegations?"

The crowd begins to surge around me and my post. The small voice is squelched and another voice enlightens me, "You are white. You are of the church. Yet you have stayed back, indeed, tried to stay invisible."

Kevin, Allan, and Vincent have left the hall, headed back to their homes in Wentworth, a so-called colored township. I stand, still firmly rooted. I overhear a woman near me, "Look. There are the others."

Two middle-aged men have been revealed by the crowd's departure. "We only knew of their release and arrival when the plane landed. Their families were only just informed," the woman explains.

Mr. Mzilikazi Khumalo and Mr. Jaki Mthetwa, imprisoned since 1979 (eleven years!) return home. No notice, no crowd, no party. A young woman approaches and embraces Mr. Khumalo. His daughter, I presume. She would have been my daughter's age, I realize, when they arrested her father.

The new voice within me urges, "You are here. You are the church's representative. You are my ambassador."

Fighting my fear and the myths that inform it, fighting my feelings of not belonging, of being an unwanted outsider, an observer only, I approach the two men and the young woman. I stretch out my hand, "Sawobona. Hello. You don't know me, but welcome home."

Their eyes seem wide with surprise and then delight as they warmly shake my hand. They do not know me, but now they know a white hand has been stretched out to them in welcome. They do not know my fear, but they do know I have stepped across invisible barriers to greet them.

Perhaps when Jesus rode into Jerusalem many in the crowd were merely spectators, wanting to see, to catch a glimpse of this controversial figure. Perhaps fear kept some in the back of the jubilant crowd, in their safe spots beside posts or up in trees, afraid of what it might mean to get involved, to be identified as "one of them."

This is what being fully alive is all about: where duty calls, even danger, to extend one's hand or allow it to be extended. This is what welcoming the Learning Spirit is all about: to experience the Now; to allow a power outside of myself to empower me, to guide me, to enable me; to fully participate in life, not to be a bystander watching from a safe spot; to stand up unreservedly in response to that voice calling me toward creative action.

The released prisoners are gone. I am left alone with my thoughts while awaiting my midnight flight to Johannesburg. I know this isn't the last time my fear will hold me back from opening myself to the Learning Spirit, from creatively reaching out to the people around me. I pray for the willingness to be more and more open to that voice calling me beyond myself into a trusting relationship and creative response to life. I pray in Paul's words:

> *Put on the full armor of God....Stand firm then, with the belt of truth buckled around your waist, with the breastplate of righteousness in place, and with your feet fitted with the readiness that comes from the gospel of peace.*
> *Ephesians 6:11a, 14, 15*

"There came a still small voice, like unto the breezes of May; and in that voice came God....Then it is that God comes; for in such spiritual sunbeams a steady blessed light is borne in upon the soul from God."[1]

Hearing this voice, opening ourselves to its call is the response of the engaged Learning Spirit.

There are three major strands of the Learning Spirit. These are *truth*, *trust*, and *creative action*, all intertwined with *willingness*.

- It is not until we comprehend a degree of *truth* about our environment and our relationship to it that genuine learning can occur.
- It is not until we can *trust* in something outside of ourselves that genuine learning can occur.
- It is only when we respond to truth and trust with *creative action* that genuine learning has occurred, that the Learning Spirit has become engaged.
- To open ourselves to *truth*, to *trust* in a power outside ourselves, and to take *creative action* all require *willingness*.

There can be no separation of these strands. They overlap, intersect, intertwine, and receive definition as the Learning Spirit only in relationship to one another.

While we can examine each strand separately, we must always bear in mind the reality of the relationship, as the genetic scientist while examining the strands of the DNA molecule must always bear in mind the intertwined and interdependent nature of the helix.

In each of us there is an ability to open up to the moment and to respond—physically, mentally, emotionally, and spiritually. When we open ourselves completely and become fully engaged with our environment, we welcome the Learning Spirit. Each event, idea, and situation informs us, and genuine learning occurs. We encounter the energy of the present moment and recognize that our life is not behind or ahead of us. It is *now*. We cease to run away from our present reality, no longer escaping into the past or the future. We are touched by truth. We accept the primacy of the Now, and in it we find eternity. We find God.

This spiritual experience, this encounter with the Learning Spirit and with God is a reality for everyone.[2] It is experienced not only by the religious, the faithful, or the seeking. Those of us who exhibit little tolerance for spiritual matters can find ourselves encountering the reality of the spirit in spite of ourselves.[3]

This encounter is similar to the sensation of a spring breeze on one's face: a presence, yet a nonpresence. Like a slight movement or a hushed whisper, the spiritual experience is easily missed or ignored. As we inhale the air we breathe, so we inhale the spirit—unknowingly, constantly, undeniably.[4]

Like the wind, the spirit has a dynamic reality yet an elusive character. Jesus describes it to Nicodemus, saying, "The wind blows wherever it pleases. You hear its sound, but you cannot tell where it comes from or where it is going. So it is with everyone born of the Spirit" (John 3:8).

No Longer Alone

Here I sit in the basement of South Shore Hospital in Chicago, in the midst of a group of strangers. What am I doing here? I know I can handle my problems on my own. I do not need any help. I just have to catch on to how they do it.

As we go around the circle, the members share not only their belief and trust in a higher power but their failures and fears, parts of human existence I have never let myself touch or feel before. "We loved you so much that we were delighted to share…our lives as well" (1Thessalonians 2:8). Through their sharing, compassion, and creative action, they emit a love that I have neither known nor experienced. It comes from them yet seems to bring out a response in me.

I realize I have always searched for answers in academic circles. I have always believed that my personal fulfillment would come through academic pursuits. But no academician has ever "loved" me as much as these strangers with whom I feel I have nothing in common. No academician has ever shared the depths of self with me, revealing fears and struggles. And I have never risked sharing my true self in an academic setting.

I feel humbled. My body, my mind, and my spirit have given out. I have been racing along the path of diplomas and success,

smack into defeat and despair. Maybe this is what I have been look-
ing for all along. A room full of strangers. No expectations. No
requirements. Just acceptance. Just unconditional acceptance and
love.
    I wonder, "Maybe I can't do it on my own. Maybe I do need
help. And maybe these people can help me."
    Their willingness to reach out to me and their willingness to
hear my pain breaks down my resistance and carries me into a
trusting attitude.
    I have never known genuine love, that urgent sharing of one-
self and questioning of another, that hungry desire to grow and to
share in another's growth, that intense dance of listening and telling. Yet here among new and unlikely colleagues I have found it.
Through their love I enter into the realm of belief and trust in a
higher power.
    I have been introduced to the theory of a higher power, of God,
on many occasions throughout my life, from childhood Sunday
school through three years of courses at a school of divinity. But
no one before has ever demonstrated the reality to me. No one has
ever shared themselves enough that their trust in a higher power
has become understandable or convincing. Now this group of
strangers introduces me to the reality of God.
    I realize I must suspend my disbelief, my preconceptions, and
my prejudices regarding the concept and experience of a higher
power. Even the word, God, has to be examined and freed from
traditional misconceptions.[5] When I suspend my preconceptions and
prejudices the doors of truth and trust open. God is revealed as a
power wanting to help me physically, emotionally, and spiritually.
Though I cannot define God, I come to believe in God. I come to
know God. My life is changed forever.
    Over the next several months, I sense love and begin to ex-
press it through working with others. In the spring of 1981, six
months after that first meeting in the hospital basement, I enter the
following declaration in my journal, "I experience a new percep-
tion of reality, a deeper understanding of the true nature of events
and feelings....I have undergone a change of direction, and conse-

quently a change in my actions, a move away from self-centered action to more creative action based upon a more altruistic motive: being of service to other people and to God."

I agree with William James "that the evidence for God lies primarily in inner personal experiences...."[6] Without this experience, God is known only by God's absence, and then to all appearances does not exist.

The essence of God is indefinable not only by ordinary people, but also by people of great faith and courageous witness. Our understanding of God is only realized to the extent of our experience of God, and ironically only to the extent that we realize our inability to obtain knowledge of God. The mystery does not lessen, but the reality, the sense of God's presence, increases.

Paul, the early Christian, describes his understanding and non-understanding of the God in whom he trusts. He writes, "Oh, the depth of the riches of the wisdom and knowledge of God! How unsearchable God's judgments, and God's paths beyond tracing out!" (Romans 11:33). God is indescribable, yet paradoxically, God can be intimately known.

The experience of the engagement of the Learning Spirit, the encounter with God, is a force that can be neither touched nor measured. The instruments of traditional science do not enhance our understanding of it. Our intellectual capacities urge us to ignore and deny it.

Spiritual pride[7] can lead us to defend a belief in the nonexistence of the spirit. We demand proofs and equations defining the capacities, the components, and the reality of God. On the other hand, we are quite comfortable with unproved theories about the physical world. We even enjoy expounding answers to puzzles of the universe before "hard data" is available. But to contemplate the existence of the immeasurable realm of the spirit remains an unacceptable proposition. In this area we suffer from tunnel vision, as if donning blinders in response to our fear of the unknown.

Yet the spirit exists.

The spirit invades us and drives us.[8] It is active and forceful, yet gentle and intimate. The sense of it, like the sensing of the breeze, is the feel of a power, a touching, a moving, a pushing, a coaxing, an urging, a calling, a grasping.[9]

We are pulled and pushed, called and sent.

The sensing of the presence of God is an essential part of the process of the engagement of the Learning Spirit. It is this sensing of a higher power and moving into a trusting relationship with this power that enables and empowers us to participate in creative action.

If we heed the whisper of truth and the nudge of the spirit, where will we be led?

The answer is articulated in the innocent-sounding words of the Jewish prophet Micah, "And what does the LORD require of you? To act justly and to love mercy and to walk humbly with your God" (Micah 6:8b). Micah calls us to radical discipleship, to sacrifice and change.

The Lay of the Land

We stand inside the dilapidated Mfanefile manse. Sunlight coming through the holes in the roof speckles the cement floor. The warm breeze blows through the empty window frames. Outside an old shed reeks of urine. There is no latrine. The nearest water supply is the small stream at the bottom of the steep ravine behind the house.

"This is where you should be living." Our friend's statement demands consideration from us.

We have assumed that since we are white we should live in the whites-only town. After all, that is the law.

Two months later, my husband, my six-month-old daughter, and I move to Mfanefile. The law...we break it and live illegally. The house...a new ceiling, two new water tanks to collect the rain water off the roof, a new latrine.

Our home is perched in the craggy hills of Zululand. Eight thousand of us live at Mfanefile, a place not mentioned on any map. It is known only as being "close to Melmoth," a town of two thousand whites, a town only nine miles away that appears on most maps.

We eight thousand depend for water on the streams cutting between the hills and whatever water tanks people have managed to install. The two thousand Melmoth residents enjoy hot and cold taps fed by a municipal reservoir. Their pools are never empty. Their flowers are never scorched.

We eight thousand are plunged into darkness with the setting of the sun. The light of a few cooking fires, flickering candles, and propane lamps escapes from our doorways. The two thousand move amid lit streets and homes exploding with lights in every room.

We eight thousand are practiced in the use of chamber pots on dark or rainy nights. The two thousand often have the choice of two or three modern bathrooms in their homes.

Tod and I are often tempted by the "rights" and privileges available to us as whites. We have access to recreational and cultural facilities such as the Melmoth swimming pool and the town library; our black African neighbors do not. We can dispose of our garbage in the Melmoth dump; our black African neighbors cannot. White residents of Melmoth have offered to us the use of their hot showers. Our neighbors never receive such offers and never expect to.

We have prayed for the willingness to stay in solidarity with our neighbors at Mfanefile. This decision has resulted in a lengthy process of learning to identify white privileges and finding the willingness not to exploit the system "just this once." So we turn in our library cards, give up use of the swimming pool, dump our garbage behind our home as our neighbors do, cease looking for social life and recreation within the white community.

The two thousand white residents of Melmoth look scornfully at Mfanefile (if they are even aware of it!) and places like it. They blame the "treacherous tendrils of poverty" or "African primitivism" or "traditionalism" or "laziness." What my eyes have seen is racism and greed that hold the blame.

Though often simplistic to the ear, the call to open ourselves to the Learning Spirit is dangerous and threatening to all that we are. The direction in which the Learning Spirit leads is often one of danger and risk, one of change and conversion/transformation, one of surrender and commitment. We are called to change our priorities, to let go of our pride and self-righteousness. We are pushed to make time and find energy to act against our own desires and to do that which seems inconvenient and often unpleasant. Our routines and expectations are sacrificed and we open ourselves to the as-yet-unknown will of God.[10]

When we open ourselves to the nudgings of the spirit, we will accept new responsibilities and obligations. We will also experience inner serenity and joy.[11]

Like the spring breeze, which we may enjoy initially with its freshness and sweetness, a light dose of the Learning Spirit can be invigorating and refreshing. But when the wind threatens to blow off our straw hats and lift our skirts, we are quick to wish the breeze away. So too with the Learning Spirit. When it invades and disrupts our lives to the extent of demanding change, we may become quite disillusioned. As Scott Peck so aptly puts it, "We are accustomed to imagining the experience of conversion or sudden call…as an 'Oh, joy!' phenomenon. In my experience, more often than not it's, at least partially, an 'Oh, shit' phenomenon."[12]

Notes

[1]Johannes Tauler, fourteenth century German Dominican mystic, cited in Stanley I. Stuber, ed., *The Christian Reader: Inspirational and Devotional Classics* (New York: Association Press, 1952), 140.

[2]See Paul Tillich, *The Eternal Now* (New York: Charles Scribner's Sons, 1963), 84.

[3]See M. Scott Peck, *The Road Less Traveled: A New Psychology of Love, Traditional Values and Spiritual Growth* (New York: Simon and Schuster, 1978), 307.

[4]See Paul Tillich, *The Eternal Now*, 86.

[5]I invite you to set aside any preconceived concepts and prejudices you hold that may distort the meanings of various terms. Except for naming the "Learning Spirit," and "creative action," I use established terms rather than create new terms. Consequently, several of the terms herein are limited by history, prejudice, popular distrust, and my own interpretation. I am not concerned so much with the terminology as with the phenomena themselves to which the terms refer.

[6]Cited in *For Today*, Overeaters Anonymous, 218.

[7]See Reinhold Niebuhr, *Faith and Politics: A Commentary on Religious, Social and Political Thought in a Technological Age* (New York: George Braziller, 1968), 77, for a discussion of spiritual pride.

[8]See John Macquarrie, *Paths in Spirituality* (Student Christian Movement Press, 1972), 41.

[9]See Richard M. Zaner, *The Disciplining of Reason's Cunning: Kurt Wolff's "Surrender and Catch."* Neuman Studies 4 (Nashville: Vanderbilt University Press, 1981), 2.

[10]See Robert McAfee Brown, *Spirituality and Liberation: Overcoming the Great Fallacy* (Philadelphia: Westminster Press, 1988), 111-112.

[11]See M. Scott Peck, *The Road Less Traveled*, 301-302.

[12]*Ibid.*, 305.

2

OBSTACLES TO THE LEARNING SPIRIT

"If we are not here, if we are not in
the present moment, fully ourselves,
we miss everything."[1]

Full Steam Ahead

My self-centeredness and fear have embittered me against my
neighbors, myself, and my God. My mind is cluttered with
the things of the world. I demand always more, quicker, faster, better. I have become greedy and focus my life's energies on accumulating gold stars and status symbols.

I harbor ingratitude that separates me from people and from
God. I am determined to be my own source of power, my own god.
I have no time to fold my hands and wait around for a god that
does not exist, or at least is not around when needed. I have rejected the image of a god that I had received as a child—the white
man bedecked in white and gold and enthroned in the clouds. I
have spent three years at a school of theology strengthening my
arguments against the existence of a god, and have emerged more
self-willed than ever.

I have been successful—academically, socially, professionally,
and financially. My life often feels centered in happiness and love,
love both from others and toward others. But I have no inclination

as to the truth, what it is or how to get it. My vision is dimmed by my fear and the myths that keep me in Plato's realm of illusory shadows. Truth is hidden from me; I trust in illusory things—academic, social, professional, and financial. My creative activities are defined by methods more reactionary and self-serving than visionary.

> *"The eye is the lamp of the body. If your eyes are good, your whole body will be full of light. But if your eyes are bad, your whole body will be full of darkness. If then the light within you is darkness, how great is that darkness!"*
>
> Matthew 6:22–23

I experience a darkness similar to the sensation of wearing sunglasses when entering a room. The room is dark, but the darkness is self-imposed. Only when reminded of the cause of the darkness do I remove the dark lenses and recognize the brilliance of the light. Only then does the light illuminate my way—even though it has been shining all along!

In the darkness, my vision is impaired. It is dimmed. Temporal achievements appear to be the "point of it all." So I go after them, full steam ahead. But I feel empty. I remain in the darkness behind my dark lenses. I shun such directives as, "Do not store up for yourselves treasures on earth, where moth and rust destroy, and where thieves break in and steal....For where your treasure is, there your heart will be also (Matthew 6:19, 21). I am on my own, and my heart has settled on things of the world. I flee from the truth and change the way an animal flees from fire.

We flee from the Learning Spirit for numerous reasons. Many of our social, religious, political, educational, and financial institutions in actuality train us to close off the Learning Spirit. They direct our focus away from the Now.

The system of apartheid actively impaired people's vision. It redirected the focus away from truth, ultimately separating people from the reality of the moment. The term *apartheid* is an Afrikaans word meaning "separation" or "setting apart." Under apartheid, people experienced life in separation from parts of themselves, from others, and from any higher power of good, i.e., God.

The experience of apartheid has been a felt part of the lives of the millions of people who live in South Africa. During the one hundred and fifty years prior to 1948, when the legal system of apartheid was instituted, the foundations of apartheid were being laid in South Africa. The people in power, initially white immigrants, developed an understanding and justification for their domination of the land, the resources, the economy, the government, and the people. They taught this understanding to their own children, and eventually to the children of those they dominated.

That understanding provided the basis for white minority domination, and continues to motivate the racist, antidemocratic movements. The racist mindset was well "taught" and well "learned." Apartheid's justification became "common knowledge." The apartheid system blocked truth for so long and so effectively that people accepted apartheid and its myths as the "truth." These include myths of superiority and inferiority, myths of industry and sloth, myths of prosperity and poverty, myths of obedience and choice, myths of death and life.[2] Apartheid, until the all-race democratic elections held on April 27, 1994, was protected by myths. The visions of the future are still heavily influenced by these same myths.

My Children Are Hungry

"Baba Shezi is here. Sifiso has died." Hearing these words we awaken, quickly pull on some clothes and go into the living room. Baba (Mr.) Shezi, a man of about forty-five years, sits on the couch crying. Tod embraces him and listens as he recites the details of his five-year-old son's death.

I remember how ten days ago Tod took little Sifiso to the hospital. Sifiso had been covered with boils. He was admitted for signs of malnourishment. Malnutrition is a common disease among the sixteen million rural black South Africans, said to be the cause of

death of 55 percent of the children who die under the age of five.[3]
Malnutrition: the hospital staff members know it well.

Five days ago, surrounded by caring nurses, Sifiso had looked better. Four days ago he had busied himself with paper and crayons, and had lovingly hugged a stuffed cat toy. He had appeared to be making a rapid recovery on a treatment of "love and food," his nurse had explained. Baba Shezi's sobs confirm that his son is yet another victim of the "disease" of malnutrition.

Preparations for the trip to the hospital morgue are made. We are joined by Sifiso's grandmother, who was his primary caregiver, and his mother who works as a domestic worker (maid) and must live away from home. His mother had returned the previous evening to visit her son, not to bury him.

Together at the hospital, we crowd into the hall outside the room where we had last seen little Sifiso. His nurse describes Sifiso's life since our last visits.

"He'd been happy," she said, "drawing, getting to know the nurses. He was a clever little boy. Yesterday his tummy swelled. We put a tube down, but nothing came up. His breathing became labored. We gave him oxygen, but as we were drawing blood for examination, his heart failed." Mother, father, and grandmother begin to cry, quietly but uncontrollably.

We proceed to the morgue, a giant icebox with concrete floors, stainless steel doors, and a heavy coolness. Sifiso lies in a pool of ice on a steel litter, dressed in the faded blue T-shirt and tan trousers he had worn from home only ten days ago.

The aide hands Tod a measuring tape to size Sifiso for his coffin; he is one meter long. "Let us pray," Tod starts. But words of prayer fail him as his crying blends into that of the Shezi family. Ma Dludla, our constant companion and interpreter, manages to pray for us all. Sifiso is returned behind the steel door.

Next task...to purchase a coffin. In the basement of the so-called "native" supermarket (owned and operated by whites) in the whites-only town of Melmoth coffins are sold. The stench of rotting potatoes permeates the air. Wooden boxes, most sized for children, line the walls. Seventy rands ($35) for a pine box with *handles...three weeks pay for Baba Shezi, whose seven other children need food. Tod pulls out his wallet...no cash...then spots his credit card. How ironic, to MasterCharge Sifiso's coffin.*

The little box fits easily into the car's trunk. Slowly we drive out of the white town, past the sugarcane fields, back to Mfanefile. The Shezis bow with gratitude as they alight from the car. Tomorrow we will collect Sifiso's body. The next day, Saturday, we will hold the funeral. Though Zionists, the Shezis appreciate the presence of an ordained minister. Sifiso will be buried on an outcrop of land near their home, a majestic spot, another irony.

I am a person of hope and have experienced God's awesome power in my life. The following lines of the psalmist ring true for me, "But as for me, I will always have hope....Since my youth, O God, you have taught me, and to this day I declare your marvelous deeds. Even when I am old and gray, do not forsake me, O God, till I declare your power to the next generation, your might to all who are to come" (Psalm 71:14,17–18). But here in South Africa I am confronted by the suffering of the people with whom Tod and I minister and the Sifisos whom we bury. "For I was hungry,...I was thirsty,...I was a stranger,...I needed clothes,...I was sick,...I was in prison..." (Matthew 25:35–36).

The messages, the myths, proclaimed by the South African whites clearly contradict the Gospel edict. Here the explanations upheld by myths are:

- *Sifiso's parents do not care. That is why his mother leaves him behind and his father drinks.*
- *Sifiso's grandmother does not care. Why else would she have waited so long to send him to the hospital?*
- *Their problem is they need family planning.*

But the reality, the truth, is quite the contrary.

- *Sifiso's parents care so much that his mother leaves her eight children behind in order to earn money for their food. His father struggles with alcoholism, working hard for five rands (about $2) per day whenever he is sober.*

- *Sifiso's aging and ailing grandmother cares so much that she has agreed to care for, as best she can, the eight children, as well as children of another son, while the parents are away finding what work and income they can.*

We can join together in prayer and action for:

- *the poor in South Africa, that they might know the empowering spirit of God;*
- *those who weep now in South Africa, that they might laugh;*
- *the people-of-color in South Africa who are hated, excluded, insulted, and rejected, that they might rejoice and know love;*
- *the rich in South Africa who are well fed now, that they might hunger for righteousness;*
- *those in South Africa who laugh now, that they might mourn and weep and repent;*
- *those who enjoy popularity within the racist regime, that they might admit their false claims to power.*

Myths block the engagement of the Learning Spirit. They distort and falsify truth. They skew the facts. The distortion and falsification result from the specific interests of those in power. Those in power, in an attempt to maintain or increase that power, establish a myth-base for themselves. They also establish a myth-base against those over whom they wield power. As power moves from one generation to the next, or from one group to the next, the myths evolve. They flourish or are extinguished as the needs of those in power change. New heros are reinforced by new myths. New events are shrouded or glorified by matching myths. New ideologies are cast in new myths.

Often myths play a harmless supportive social and political role. For example, in accounts of George Washington chopping down the cherry tree and Johnny Appleseed's trek across the territories, American folklore is forged. These tales, based upon historical accounts, are recognized as acceptable propaganda, as exaggerations, as folklore, as myths.

However, when a society such as South Africa (or the United States) acts unjustly and oppresses numbers of its citizens, the interpretation of history and the creation of social and political myths can prove harmful and destructive, even fatal. As Paul writes, "For the time will come when [people] will not put up with sound doctrine. Instead, to suit their own desires, they will gather around them a great number of teachers to say what their itching ears want to hear. They will turn their ears away from the truth and turn aside to myths" (2 Timothy 4:3–4). Nations defend themselves and destroy their enemies through the use of these social myths.

Blind Faith

"Zulus who join the ANC are misled."

I try to listen calmly as Dumisani, a clean-cut professional man, spews out his well-learned propaganda. But my thoughts are boiling!

His comfortable BMW gingerly progresses over the steep rocky road cut into the mountain in this lonely place. I want only to reach my parked car at the kraal at the crest. I try to be grateful for his help; my Toyota will not clear the boulders that fill this homemade roadbed.

"We Zulus will never be led by a Xhosa. They burn everything they see." Behind my calm look, I remember my Xhosa colleague at Inanda Seminary and her tidy apartment.

Dumisani has learned his lines well, but when pressed for details he can offer no support for his broad claims, and only repeats them louder.

The colorful language of this member of Inkatha's inner cabinet depicts Nelson Mandela (a Xhosa) and "his Xhosa ANC" as monsters ready to kill children in their sleep. On the other hand, Dumisani's words spread a warm powerful aura around his beloved leader, Mangasuthu Buthelezi, Chief Minister of the Zulu homeland, KwaZulu. KwaZulu, a land and a position created and maintained by the white government in Pretoria...a fact Dumisani seems quick to forget.

"The Xhosas come to Nseleni [a Zulu township north of Durban] in the dark of night and break into houses and kill Zulus," *he explains.* *I recall a recent conversation with a concerned deacon in the church we serve at Nseleni. Our deacon, a Zulu, had expressed his anger at the Inkatha* Zulus *who came by night and terrorized ANC-supporting* Zulus.
I smile, thank Dumisani for the lift, and gratefully tumble into my car.
The next week I read in The Weekly Mail *newspaper:*

32 Inkatha men held after attacking village:...*Armed with guns, cane knives, knobkerries and assegais, they were arrested hours after an attack on the settlement of kwaZini [a Zulu community] that left homes razed to the ground and resulted in the death of a school principal....Inkatha, however, faces much embarrassment over the arrests....The arrest of the 32 [Inkatha supporters] lends weight to claims that Inkatha is either acting in bad faith or has little control over its followers....Residents claim that there were as many as 100 assailants, who burnt the homes after pillaging them,...stole cattle and destroyed much of kwaZini's cane crop. The residents fled but Khosa, who was on crutches due to an accident, was unable to escape and was hacked to death. He had been accused by Inkatha people of harbouring ANC refugees....After the arrest of the 32, the remainder...continued its rampage, burning down a further five homes.[4]*

I wonder if Dumisani has heard this news. I wonder if he has found a way to explain away this atrocity. I wonder if he will ever want to hear the truth about Inkatha.

———

Myths play on our loyalties, our fears, and our greed. When we are distracted by myths, we engage ourselves in our reality in only a limited capacity and the Learning Spirit is obstructed. As a result, our vision narrows and the light of the spirit is kept out. Our blindness enables us to uphold and defend falsehoods and myths about our society and our relationship to it. Our blindness convinces us to maintain things as they are.

For example, in South African history and folklore, Shaka the Zulu king is portrayed as extremely violent and egocentric. These accounts have been manipulated causing them to become separated from their historic and folklore qualities. They have been forged into propaganda that produces generalizations about *all* Zulus, past and present. During the years following the release of Nelson Mandela, these generalizations were frequently recounted side-by-side with news accounts and photographs of violence perpetrated by Zulus. Zealous descriptions of "black on black" violence perpetrated by "half-naked Zulu men, wielding swords and shields," conjured up the Shaka myth, the Zulu myth. This played on people's racially based fears and directly influenced the interpretation of pre-election events. Consequently, the generalizations significantly harmed the image of the black African community.

These myths, and others, have promoted such theories as black primitivism and white supremacy, which were substantiated under apartheid by the government, the media, the schools, and often religion. The only purpose of the phrase, "black on black violence," coined by journalists, is to promote racist myths. There is no equivalent phrase, "white on white violence," for it is meaningless, whether in Ireland, Bosnia, or the suburbs of Boston. We assume two groups of whites in conflict have substantial reason, that their skin color alone cannot fully explain their conflict. The assumption, the myth, underlying the phrase "black on black" is that people with dark skin need no other reason for violence; their color, their race, explains it.

A Stone's Throw

The LORD *said, "What have you done? Listen! Your brother's blood cries out to me from the ground."*

Genesis 4:10

"I've never been so frightened in my life!" Marjorie's gaze moves to the fence behind her home. *"They were right there. The guns were so loud, deafening. I knew Joe was with them."* She has been showing us the crocheted items she and the refugee women residing in the school hall are making.

"It happened right in the midst of the funeral," Joe explains. He grows stern. *"The funeral was for two of the refugees who had been staying here on campus. The two men were killed when they traveled to a meeting to plan the return of their families to their homes. Their families are still here. We were a great crowd, gathered for their memorial service. The police and army troops also had come. They stood outside the school, on the other side of the fence...heavily armed...ready for action. I felt their eyes on us as we entered the chapel."*

"It seemed the service had barely begun when there were gunshots. A student rushed in and announced that someone had been killed at the school gate." Joe looks tired. He has been working hard as principal of a theological seminary in Imbali, a township in the midst of the violence.

Joe continues, *"The body was beyond the gate, a gaping wound in the chest. People gathering around the boy were being 'controlled' by the police and army, all in combat gear."*

Marjorie shudders at the recollection of the war scene. She crochets a green bed-sock as her husband continues.

"When I confronted the Lieutenant, he took full credit for the kill. He insisted that the dead boy had acted in a dangerously threatening manner. That boy was only about fifteen years old! How dangerous could he have been with his sticks and stones?" Joe's voice shakes. *"Then, without any audible orders, a volley of assault rifle and shot gun fire was loosed over our heads. I've never been so angry! Those shots might easily have provoked the already upset crowd. Luckily, everyone just fled."*

After lunch Joe invites us for a stroll across the quiet campus. Five-year-old Amy had gone out earlier to play. Now we spot her in the field. She has already befriended several of the refugee children and is engaged in their play.

Only as we draw nearer do we comprehend their "game." The children have divided into sides, the UDF/ANC (United Democratic Front and African National Congress) versus Inkatha. They are acting out the battles of their older sisters and brothers and parents. Small stones zip across the field between them.

I wonder, "Would the media still try to call this 'black on black' violence even though a white child is involved?" Amy, a gentle little girl, probably like most of the other girls in the "game," isn't playing because of her color, her class, her ethnicity, her tribe, or her nation. Amy has joined in the rumble because she has chosen to play the "game."

Those whom the children mimic have not killed because of their color, their ethnicity, their tribe, or their nation. They have joined in the violence because they have chosen that means to strive toward their goal. It is not "black on black" violence, it is the violence of one human being against another, one child of God against another.

We reach the field and break up the "game." Children drop their stones and their interest turns to the nearby slide. Amy comes away with a red welt on her forearm which she rubs the remainder of the day. She does not complain or cry. Tears are not part of the "game."

To use the word white *to describe my daughter tells you nothing. Having light skin does not make her think a certain way, learn a certain way, live a certain way, or play a certain way. To use the word* black *to describe my daughter would tell you just as much.*

Racist myths and generalizations become the ideology of the dominant group and often the ideology of the victimized and oppressed group(s).

Betrayal

"There is nothing that I can do for you. I am just a social worker," Mrs. Zwane sits behind the massive wood desk. I face

her, wedged between Mrs. Miyeza, a neighbor from Mfanefile, and my interpreter, Ma Dludla.

"There is nothing that I can do for you." Her judgment of the case is stated. It seems more like a prejudgment freeing her from further responsibilities by hurtling an Herculean task at us. The future closes in around Mrs. Miyeza as she is reprimanded by Mrs. Zwane, "You came to me last year. I told you what to do then. If your husband has disappeared, you must find him or have the police prove he can't be found."

Mrs. Miyeza's sentence is formidable: spend money she does not have to travel a day's journey to Nkandla to ask police officers there, whom she does not know, to try to find her husband who disappeared from their district two years ago.

"Can't she file the missing person report here, and have it sent on to the Nkandla district?" I ask.

"No. She must go there," Mrs. Zwane replies.

"Can't someone else, someone who is at Nkandla, file the report there for her?" I inquire.

"No. She must go herself," the reply is firm.

"Why didn't you notify Mrs. Miyeza of this when she first inquired of you?" I ask exasperated. "She's been waiting eighteen months for your answer."

"First I asked her for the birth certificates of her five children. When she brought them in she knew what else was needed. Does she think we just give child support grants to anyone? She must prove her husband can't be found, and only a letter from the police where he disappeared will suffice. She knows," Mrs. Zwane retorts, her eyes glaring at me over the broad desk.

I think of Mrs. Miyeza beside me. Does a person who "knows" what to do wait eighteen months to do it? Does a person who "knows" how to get financial support wait eighteen months with her five children out of school? With her five children hungry?

Mrs. Zwane's short trunk holds her head just above the edge of her desk as she sits seemingly protected by the desk's massive bulk. She seems miles away, separated from us not only by the desk but also by an icy chill. My heart begins to harden against her.

*This same Mrs. Zwane is a parishioner in my congregation.
She, like Mrs. Miyeza, is a black African. She, unlike Mrs.
Miyeza, lives in a comfortable house. Mrs. Zwane has accepted employment with the South African Government's Office of Bantu Affairs.
Her fluency in English, Afrikaans, and Zulu makes her ideal for
dealing with the problems of black Africans living in white-con-
trolled areas.*

The tragedy is that Mrs. Zwane is clearly working for *the white
government, and* against *the black Africans who approach her for
assistance. Each day she has the opportunity to help or hinder
black Africans in their attempts to get needed assistance. As in
Mrs. Miyeza's case, Mrs. Zwane often hands out impossible tasks,
when she could apply creative ideas to some of the problems and
overcome or overstep others completely.*

*I have sat silently while Mrs. Zwane has reiterated the list of
feats Mrs. Miyeza must accomplish in order to get her financial
assistance. My anger boils. How can Mrs. Zwane be so insensitive
to the plight of her black African sister? Where is Mrs. Miyeza going
to find the money for the "necessary" journey to Nkandla? Who is
going to look after Mrs. Miyeza's five children while she is away?
Who is going to represent a poor black African woman in soiled
clothes and bare feet to the towering prejudice of the South African
Police? My rage explodes in English. I spill out my concerns.*

*Now it is Mrs. Zwane's turn to listen. She listens silently, then
gently suggests, "Let's ask Mrs. Miyeza what she thinks. The solution to this problem shouldn't be our solution; it should be hers."*

*To Mrs. Zwane's surprise and my delight, Mrs. Miyeza, who
has not understood a word of my English outburst, boldly begins
to voice the same concerns. "Who will watch my children? Where
will I get the money? I'm afraid of the police."*

*It is Mrs. Zwane's turn to be angry. She pounds her fist on the
massive desk that divides us, and like a broken record she begins
again, "If you want your aid money, then you must do these
things...."*

*Ma Dludla, my interpreter, starts to laugh. Mrs. Miyeza and I
join in her laughter. Mrs. Zwane stops her tirade and, so as not to*

look a fool, laughs, too. But she will start her explanation again when the laughter ceases, expecting Mrs. Miyeza to fall into line in the normal way.

What myths make Mrs. Zwane harden against her black African brothers and sisters? What lines of the system has she bought that close off her own ability to act creatively? Lines like:

- *You cannot give money to just anyone.*
- *You cannot trust "them." Mrs. Miyeza probably has a new husband at home.*
- *It is really not my problem.*

Perhaps I should pity Mrs. Zwane. What can she do? Perhaps if she gives out too much money the white magistrate will be upset with her, perhaps even fire her.

No, Mrs. Zwane will not get my pity. She has chosen her role in the system. The red tape she has placed before Mrs. Miyeza is not necessarily the result of the bureaucracy, but is just as likely the result of her own decisions, the result of the bureaucrat. The Herculean hurdles—of cost, time, inaccessibility, distance, language—are enforced by the workers in the system, and are usually accepted as "the way it is" by those who are the victims.

For Mrs. Zwane and other civil servants, co-option may appear to be a soft option, but its way is full of deceit and unkindness.

Apartheid promoted limited vision and, too often, self-serving destructive action by its people, both white and black. One method of perpetuating this limited vision was to create a comfortable black African middle class, of which Dumisani and Mrs. Zwane are part. This same portion of the population was subtly persuaded, and sometimes blatantly encouraged, to accept the myths of the status quo and to be fully co-opted into the apartheid scheme.[5]

Apartheid and its supporting myths effectively short-circuited genuine education, as truth is a necessary component in genuine learning. Millions of people, black and white, remained resigned to an evil system that controlled their every movement. They came to accept apartheid as "the way it is," even as God's will.

Sweater Secrets

"I planted the six seed beds today," Sarie announces proudly. She has been telling us stage by stage of the progress. First the digging of the compost pit six months before. Then the filling of it, layer by layer alternating refuse from her home and cut grass from her expansive yard. Earlier this week she informed us that the six beds were dug, the compost spread, and today...the seeds are planted. Her joy and contentment at seeing a job through to its completion are contagious, for a moment.

Sarie has undertaken a lot in her new home: repainting the interior, tearing down walls and putting up others, fencing in the large plot, laying a stone walk and a brick drive, erecting new cages for her ducks and chickens, and creatively landscaping with a display of hedges and flowers. Sarie has undertaken a lot, and the results are beautiful. Now a six-bed vegetable garden is nestled in the corner of her yard. She and her family will be happy there for many years.

"I'm pleased with all I've done, and I thank God for all the blessings I have." Sarie returns to her desk.

Yes, hard work does pay off, and Sarie's industriousness has made her house what it is today. And, yes, Sarie can thank God for her beautiful home and vegetable beds.

But Sarie herself never planted those seed beds. She never dug them. She never painted her house. She never laid a brick. Black African workers did.

Sarie owns three shops. Many times I drive past her new home and witness "her" shop staff on their knees in "her" garden, or laying bricks in "her" drive. I witness "her" maid emptying the refuse onto the compost pile.

I recall a poem by a South African woman:

> *My heart cries out within me as I watch*
> *Affluent whites go by*

Well clothed, well fed, secure
Within their circle,
Privilege.
How many care, or even think
Of those
Deprived by their very having?...
The others walking by—
Non-citizens, non-people,
Called non-whites—
They understand too well.
Theirs is a daily knowledge,
Part of life,
A constant pain and anguish
Like a knife
Which turns within their hearts...[6]

The riches of this country, enjoyed by the whites, have been paid for by the sweat and often the lives of black Africans. Employees are often closer to slaves than free workers. "Oh, don't worry, 'my girl' can do it," and the cashier is told to babysit or make tea. The stockperson is handed a shovel and told to dig a garden bed.

No, God did not give that home to Sarie; money and the sweat of black African workers did.

No, God did not give that money and those workers to Sarie; greed did.

Sarie has given me a beautiful hand-knitted sweater. She even let me choose the yarn from her well-stocked chest. I have always been impressed by the quantities of knitted articles she manages to pump out.

Soon after the vegetable beds are dug, I enter her dry goods shop. She is instructing an employee on a knitting technique. Upon seeing me, Sarie's face lights up. She takes the needles and the yarn out of the employee's hands and beams, "Isn't this a lovely sweater I'm knitting for my husband?"

I return home, find the sweater Sarie gave to me, and give it away. I wonder who knitted it.

Though grace is shown to the wicked,
   they do not learn righteousness;
even in a land of uprightness they go on doing evil
   and regard not the majesty of the LORD.

                              Isaiah 26:10

———————

Our security and comfort can lull us into complacency. If we are not suffering, we do not tend to find any urgency to examine our behavior and values. We become lazy and exist in a cloud of rationalization, closed to the Learning Spirit.

We may be pulled by personal greed or tribal loyalties and animosities. We may hunger for power and privilege or be lulled by seemingly secure comforts. In each case, our ability to open ourselves fully to see the truth of the world around us and to welcome the Learning Spirit is severely limited.

Partial or total disengagement from our environment is not usually a conscious decision on our part. It is most often the automatic response mechanism instilled through years of socialization and training.

Double Standards

"Have you read this new book about time management?" Jill asks me. "It's been a revelation for me."

Jill always seems a bit frantic. Her scaly cheeks and hands silently witness to her nervous nature. She always seems to be on the run and is usually worried about one thing or another.

"I always race around," she confides. "What I need is to take a regular break. This book calls it taking a Sabbath. No exceptions. No interruptions. Actually getting away each week for a day or even half a day to unwind, to relax, to pray. The author explains how to arrange one's work to make room for this weekly Sabbath. He claims it's essential."

Jill's position as codirector of a church retreat center has weighed heavily on her these past two years. It is exciting to hear her speak of resting and taking time for her own needs.

The day is beautiful and clear. We enjoy flying the kite with the children, and then head into the center's communal dining hall for lunch.

Jill begins to explain the new rotation system for the kitchen staff: eleven-day shifts. Because the black African staff live on the grounds for the duration of their shifts, this plan would presumably decrease tardiness and would add more stability one day to the next, so Jill explains.

I ask, "When is their *Sabbath?"*

Jill's egocentricity has distorted the universal truth of oneness, and has made me *fundamentally different from* you. *According to her perception, her needs are sacred and "they" have no needs, unless she determines them. Jill needs her Sabbath, but the staff members need to serve on an eleven-day shift. Jill, failing to achieve a universal vision, substitutes her partial prejudices for the universal values she lacks.*

Apartheid enabled people to uphold the myths of dominance and superiority. The racism, fear, and greed effectively separated people, both physically and emotionally. The prejudice apartheid upheld, and which still exists, destroys any universal vision for humanity.

The apostle John, writing to the church of Laodicea, captures the essence of this dilemma: "You say, 'I am rich; I have acquired wealth and do not need a thing.' But you do not realize that you are wretched, pitiful, poor, blind and naked" (Revelation 3:17). Why have so many whites claimed their dominance and wealth as God's will for them? Why have so many black Africans accepted their poverty and oppression as God's will for them?

We must become aware of the ideologies we hold. We must consider the way our ideologies create and maintain our dependent relationship with those in power or our own positions of power.

I Never Realized

We have worked together on several workshops, she in charge, me assisting. I look up to her, sensing in her both a profound wisdom and a steady faith. We have laughed together, been serious together, cried together. We are friends.

"I'm tired of being on display. There's so much racism," her words startle me. "Children want to touch me because they've never seen a real black person before."

I am silent.

"There have been good times, but I don't want to face white racism from brothers and sisters in the church anymore, at least not on a regular basis when I don't have to. I'm not going to do any more workshops."

"But I never realized..." my reply drifts off. I recognize in that moment that I have been part of the problem, for I never realized—never realized what subtleties have pained my friend, never realized the bruising she has endured, never realized the hardships of being black in the Northeast United States. I feel ashamed.

A letter written to me in 1989 by my white sister-in-law comes to mind. She writes:

> *Your letter opened my eyes to every old racism lurking in the corners and sometimes the central corridors of my life. Lately I've seen how racism manifests as a complete blind spot in a person's life. At [the seminary I attend], one of its [racism's] insidious forms is a lack of interest or effort in getting to know African-American brothers and sisters. I have seen whites sit down at a cafeteria table by me and a fellow African-American student and proceed to engage only me in conversation. I also see men do this with women by having eye contact and addressing only the other man or men in the group. The women are left to uncomfortably let their eyes roam here or there. I have been experimenting with interrupting this dynamic. It's ironic that this has only now appeared so blatantly, when it had been happen-*

ing all my life, but I'd just taken it for granted and not allowed myself to notice it." [7]

Since my return from South Africa, I have re-installed my protective shields and rehung my cultural blinders. By the nature of my race and class, I have stepped quietly into the shoes of the powerful and have lost contact with the oppressed of my society. In Mfanefile, South Africa, I woke up white in a black world. I woke up wealthy in a poor world. By the nature of my race and class, I was the exception; I woke up powerful and aware of my power amidst the powerless and impoverished. Now in North America I wake up white in a white world. I wake up middle-class in a middle-class world. I am no longer the exception, but one of many. By the nature of my race and class, I wake up powerful, and my awareness is dulled. My friend wakes up black in a white world. By the nature of her race and class, waking up and moving around in the world has consequences "I never realized."

I recall a quote, the source of which I do not know, "All that is necessary for the forces of evil to succeed in this world is for enough good men and women to do [and realize] nothing." God, forgive my blindness and my ignorance.

Only when we become aware of our own complicity in our culture's structures of power and dependency can we move away from our patterns of thought and behavior that uphold these structures. Only when we become willing to examine our attitudes and fears about race, poverty, religion, spirituality, work, economics, politics, and education do we become open to the Learning Spirit. Only then does dramatic change become a possibility, in ourselves and in our society.

One of the greatest obstacles to the engagement of the Learning Spirit is the lack of trust and the sense of powerlessness that becomes manifested as fear. We fear many things, including loss, insecurity, uselessness, and change. Fear and our sense of powerlessness can be most profound when we confront death.

Sweet, Sweet Death

*It has rained almost constantly for forty-eight hours. The roads
are slippery with mud. Everyone seems chilled by the damp cold.
I need to discuss Mandla's test results with Dr. Hall and get
him started on a course of medication, so I decide to try to make it
to the hospital today.*

*Having parked the Toyota near the Nene's home at the top of
our steep grade, I ascend the hill, Mandla on my back. I maneuver
my way up the slick slope, managing to stay erect.*

*I wave appreciatively to Mrs. Nene. Coming towards me, she
calls out, "Baba's spitting blood again. We've just called Billy to
take him to the hospital. His truck will make it through this mud."*

*I instruct Mandla to wait in the car while I accompany Mrs.
Nene. Baba Nene recognizes me as I pass the small open window
of his hut, and he greets me, "Umfundisi wami."*

*I've always felt a special tenderness toward this man. My son
has his name—Mandlenkosi. Baba Nene has always called me re-
spectfully, "Umfundisi wami," "My minister." No female deriva-
tive, full acceptance and respect for me as an ordained minister, as
his ordained minister. We've shared communion in his home. We've
seen his son through a leg amputation due to an industrial accident. Baba Nene supervised the building of our rondoval. He had
come back to church after many years away. Just on Monday he
had said, "I never forget you, Umfundisi wami. You get my pension. You help my wife's son. I never forget you."*

*Billy arrives. Four of us lift Baba Nene from his bed. I hold his
thin bony legs. He says loudly, "Can't walk," in English, as if to
me alone.*

"I'm going to the hospital anyway. I'll take him." I offer.

*We set him in the back seat with Mrs. Nene beside him to keep
him from falling over. I buckle up Mandla in the front seat beside
me, and I drive off.*

*In the rearview mirror, I see Baba Nene slip away. Mrs. Nene
has not realized he has gone. But I hear his moans cease. I see the
eyes rest. I see the throat still. I see him slip away, and I wonder
where he has gone.*

I rush through the hospital gate crying, "Emergency!" Two nurses lift Baba Nene onto a cart. I lift Mandla out of the car and hold him close. By the time I get inside Dr. Hall knows. "He was already gone," she says. "The hospital policy," she continues, "states clearly that when a person is dead on arrival, we are not to accept the body, that it must be removed from the hospital premises."

Aghast and horrified, I whisper, "You mean I have to put him back in the car and take him home? What will I do with him? And little Mandla will be in the car. Think of the health hazard!"

"I realize the dilemma this policy puts people in, and I refuse to obey it," Dr. Hall's words calm me. "I just want you to know what the rules are. I've written 'extremitis on arrival,' but he was already gone when you arrived. I agree, for safety's sake, the body must stay here."

"Thanks," I breathe a sigh of relief. "I'll have to tell his wife."

I kneel, one hand around Mandla, the other around Mrs. Nene. "He's gone."

She is quiet. She had known he was dying since his hospital visit two weeks ago. I set Mandla on a chair while Mrs. Nene and I go to look at Baba Nene. I roll back the grey blanket. She nods, "Enough."

I fetch from the car the blanket we brought for Baba Nene, and wrap her in it. She will stay wrapped in it until after her husband is buried.

I return to my son. Dr. Hall examines him and prescribes tablets for whooping cough.

Baba Nene's best friend arrives, the grandfather of my children's best friends, our neighbor. "I have bad news." I hold him. "He's gone."

Tears fill his eyes. No, he does not want to see the body. He sits quietly in the back of the waiting room. His crinkled face, reflecting eighty-two years of life, looks old and worn. His bent and cracked hands finger his hat between his knees. His yellow slicker drips persistently onto the linoleum floor.

I return, Mandla at my side, to the small room in which Baba Nene lies. "These are Baba Nene's toes," Mandla states as he reaches up on tippy-toe to touch the blanket draped over the cold toes of Baba Nene.

"Yes, those are Baba Nene's toes," I continue with my task, measuring Baba Nene's body for the coffin. One hundred and eighty-five centimeters; he is a tall man. I wonder where he went when he died. Where is his spirit now, as his body lies here getting cold?

The metal cart arrives to transport the body to the morgue. I wonder where Baba Nene is, where he will be when his old and broken body becomes a sheet of ice.

His dying face haunts me. I realize someday it will be my face, relaxed and still. And where will I be?

"Yes, Mandla, those are Baba Nene's toes. But he's gone."

Death...to be seen, touched, smelled. To be pondered and accepted with all its mystery. Death...the inevitable destiny for us all, yet often an unwelcome visitor.

In the "First World" experience, we are, in life, often severed from the reality of death. Death has become the realm of professionals: morticians, hospital chaplains, funeral directors. It has lost its rightful place in our experience of the cycle of life. It has become an unknown experience: untouched, unseen, unsmelled. The mystery of death and our fear of death have been magnified by our isolation from it.

Contact with the dying and with the dead can provide transforming educational experiences. This contact can enable us to find acceptance of death as part of the lives of others and as part of our own lives. This acceptance can then, in turn, enable us, free us, to carry on with life. "Throughout the whole of life one must continue to learn to live, and what will amaze you even more, throughout life one must learn to die,"[8] proclaimed the Roman statesman Seneca.

Living with death we are freed for life. Admitting our own powerlessness over death, we can be empowered to live more fully.

Our spirits, emboldened by trust, can see the true circumstances of death and can be freed to become engaged in creative reflection and action.

When we are open to the stirrings of the Learning Spirit, we will clearly see the myths and fears that shroud our perspective. We will overcome the obstacles in our path and live fully in the Now. We will desire truth and will embrace freeing attitudes of trust. We will experience the everydayness of life through the lenses of the spirit, with a critical mind and a compassionate heart. When we engage the Learning Spirit, our lives will be transformed. Our lives will be guided by a higher power toward truth, trust, and creative action.

Notes

[1]Thich Nhat Hanh, "Enjoying Peace," *Fellowship* (New York: Fellowship of Reconciliation, 1990), 8-9.

[2]See Marianne Cornevin, *Apartheid: Power and Historical Falsification* (Paris: UNESCO, 1980) in which Cornevin examines ten myths upheld in South Africa. She provides the South African version of the myths and refutes them one by one, establishing a different set of truths. See also Julian Burgess, Esau duPlessis, et al, *The Great White Hoax: South Africa's International Propaganda Machine* (London: Africa Bureau, 1977) in which the relationship between propaganda and myths in South Africa is examined.

[3]See Roger Omond, *The Apartheid Handbook: A Guide to South Africa's Everyday Racial Policies* (Middlesex, England: Penguin Books, Ltd., 1985), 80.

[4]"32 Inkatha Men Held After Attacking Village," *The Weekly Mail* (Durban, South Africa), Oct. 26-Nov. 1, 1990, sec. 1, p. 1.

[5]See Sampi Terreblanche, "The Brotherhood Syndrome: the Origins of Favoritism," *Sash: Focus on Corruption* 33 (Mowbry, South Africa: Black Sash, Sept. 1989), 10.

[6]"My Heart Cries Out," by Helen Kotze, cited in John De Gruchy, ed., *Cry Justice: Prayers, Meditations and Readings from South Africa*, 112. "My Heart Cries Out" was originally published in 1974.

[7]Cheri Pierre Dale, letter to author, December 19, 1989.

[8]Cited in M. Scott Peck, *The Road Less Traveled*, 74-75.

3

THE LEARNING SPIRIT HELIX: WILLINGNESS

There is nothing in our power except
that which is present while we
are willing.
—St. Augustine of Hippo[1]

Not My Kid!

The sounds of children permeate the air. They stand, all eight hundred of them, like cattle in a corral. Their matching uniforms create a contrasting pattern of black and white against the tan buildings. Then... silence. I watch in wonder, protected from view by the lace curtains in my window. I think to myself, "Wouldn't teachers in the United States be impressed with this silence so easily attained?!"

A few words of a single voice waft toward me. Then a magnificent chorus! The Zulu words of the Lord's Prayer rise to greet the morning. School has begun.

The Mfanefile Elementary School sits within a guava's throw of my home. I have walked through the ten classrooms. I have seen the wooden benches, the broken window panes, and the leaky metal roofs. I have seen two hundred children crammed into the small church sanctuary, managing to arrange themselves into three additional class groups. I have seen the primitive outhouse and have smelled the reek of urine along the paths.

My mind wanders to my five-year-old daughter. I was not ready for her request of a week ago.

"Why can't I go to school with my friends?" Amy had asked. We have lived at Mfanefile for more than four years. We have thought about Amy's schooling many times. As an educator, I am convinced formal schooling is not essential for education, but both Tod and I recognize that school is an integral part of most modern societies. We know, for political and ideological reasons, we will not send her to the white school in Melmoth. Yet we are also unwilling to send her to the Mfanefile School. Now we are faced with making a decision.

My fears surface. Amy will be the only white at the school. What if Amy gets teased or beaten up just because she is white? What if teachers favor her and cause resentment from other students? I am obsessed by visions of Amy coming home bruised and bloody, by visions of her getting pregnant as a teenager and never going to college, of her sacrificing her future—the one I expect of her.

My fears harden my resolve. No way am I going to let my kid go to this Third World school that could be featured in National Geographic Magazine!

The chorus ends. Thembi and Malindi, two of Amy's closest friends, eagerly work their way to the front of the line as the eight hundred students file into the classrooms. A teacher's voice rings out clearly, "Good morning, class."

My resolve weakens. I feel torn. I have always believed attending public school to be a justice issue: schooling is a right to be shared among all people, not a privilege to be claimed by a few. But now it is my own kid under consideration, and my judgment clouds. What message will we be telling Amy if we say she is different, if we say she deserves special privileges, if we say this school is not good enough for her? What will we be saying to our neighbors—we will use the privilege of our race and wealth to send our child elsewhere because Mfanefile is not good enough? Half of the world's children attend schools like this. Why not mine? Why am I unwilling to send her? What better education can we offer to her?

Then, as if scales have fallen from my eyes, everything becomes clear. I become willing. I realize—we live here; this is our school; this is Amy's school.

My racism, my classism, and my elitism have blocked the clarity of my understanding and have made me unwilling. My racism sees only black and white and projects Amy being beaten up because of her color. My classism stands repulsed at the conditions of the buildings, the lack of supplies, the size of the class groups. My elitism considers graduating from an Ivy League University the only meaningful goal of Amy's schooling, and considers a "proper" education a requirement for success. My own ambitions do not allow me to even begin to consider Amy happily attending school here at Mfanefile, her home.

For the next year, Amy Thandiwe Gobledale attends first grade at the Mfanefile Elementary School. Her teacher, Miss Nonhla Mkhulise, welcomes her warmly and treats her fairly. Her class of sixty-four students meets in the crowded sanctuary. She often takes our bucket and mop to clean up the classroom after a rain. During the noon recess our home resounds with the gleeful laughter of Amy and her friends, their uniforms creating black and white patterns in the sunlight. And each morning, as I watch from my window, I lose track of Amy as she gathers as one of the eight hundred and joins the chorus.

Baba wethu, Osezulwini...Our Father, who art in heaven, hallowed be thy name. Thy kindgom come. Thy will be done....

———

An imperative of the Learning Spirit is willingness. While truth, trust, and creative action are the strands that form the helix of the Learning Spirit, willingness is like a mesh through which the strands weave. We do not fully encounter truth without willingness. We do not fully move into trust or fully experience conversion without willingness. And we do not undertake creative action without willingness.

Willingness is the state of being open to the unknown, of trusting in the unknowable, of acting in the face of great risk and sacrifice. Willingness is neither observable nor measurable; willingness is felt. It is an internal experience known only to the individual experiencing it and understood only in terms of the attitudes and actions accompanying it. Willingness is an experience into which we move or are moved. It is the inner experience that precedes both choice and decision.[2]

A Priceless Gift

The rains have finally stopped, and the South African sun is shining brilliantly. Uprooted trees lie across our road. Leaves torn from their stems litter the ground. What an irony that in the midst of this destruction we have a service of thanksgiving.

I greet the people at the church door—Mrs. Shandu who lost her bedroom in the flood, Mrs. Ngema who lost her kitchen, Mr. Mkwanazi who lost everything but the clothes and blanket he wears today. Twenty-five of us gather to give thanks to God that the torrential rains have passed and that everyone in our community is safe. We gather to receive emergency relief money that has come from the church because the government relief has been insufficient.

I glance at the stack of envelopes on our worship table, the relief money to be distributed. Money to help our families rebuild and refurnish their mud and pole homes that were washed away. Money to buy new seed needed to replant ruined crops.

I open the service with prayer. We read from Genesis of the end of the flood. Prayers and songs arise from the congregation as each person receives a plain white envelope containing two hundred rands, about $80.00, more money than any of them would usually see at one time. Each twenty-rand note is as much as any one person might have in a month.

Someone reminds me that it is time for the offering. The basket is not passed, but sits on the central table to enable each person to truly "bring" their offering of thanks to the Lord. Joyfully, even tearfully, each person comes forward stepping to the rhythm of a song.

I sit. And, a bit awestruck, I watch. I hear the coins clink against one another in the basket. Then Nokukhanya Dludla, a widow and mother of eight, approaches the table.

I recollect my recent visit to Ma Dludla's home—pieces of metal roofing covering the holes in the mud walls, one piece held in place by a battered and water-swollen trunk; heaps of wrinkled clothes and rusting cooking utensils salvaged from the two rooms that had been destroyed; mounds of caked mud on the floor where the rain had washed down the walls.

I remember when Ma Dludla brought the list of those whose homes had suffered damage from the heavy rains, how her name was missing. "Ma, your name's not here. You had two rooms washed away," I had said. "Umfundisi, these others need the money more than I do," had been her willing response. I added her name to the list.

Ma Dludla pauses before the offering basket. From her dress pocket pokes the handkerchief in which she keeps her coins for offering. But rather than reach for a coin she opens her envelope and pulls out a twenty-rand note, a tithe, enough money to feed her family for a week, enough money to buy candles for five months, enough money for ten visits to the doctor. As a congregation we have discussed tithing as a way to show God our thanks. But I have been speaking more to the well-to-do, not to the poor. She folds the money carefully.

Because Ma Dludla is facing the front where I am sitting, only I can see. I start to reach out to stop her, to tell her a coin is suffi-cient, to say that her tithe is too much, to say that she who has so little should not be so generous. But I stop myself, or perhaps it would be better to say that I am stopped. The joy Ma Dludla feels, her thankfulness and her love for God fill the moment, a priceless moment. This poor widow, this very poor woman, willingly gives out of her poverty and thanksgiving.

For people who think of others first, for cultures based on com-munity rather than competition and individualism, sharing is sec-

ond nature. For Ma Dludla, the expression of her thanksgiving, her tithe, is an obvious action for her, a person of faith and love. Ma Dludla shares in spite of the needs of her family. She gives because she understands the bottom line: all that we have and are comes from God, and she is thankful!

For us who care first about number one, these acts of love and thanksgiving seem excessive, and we can feel threatened by them if we really take the time to understand that we are called to this, too. When we do consider our responsibility to others, we tend to get caught in a rut of "should" behavior: I should give more food to the hungry, I should put more money in the plate, I should, we should.

When we become truly thankful for that which we have and that which we are, when we direct our thanks and trust to the Spirit that created and sustains us, then we are freed from all the "shoulds." When we become truly thankful, our eyes begin to see more clearly the hunger, poverty, and suffering around us today. When we become truly thankful, our arms and feet are put into motion, not out of a sense of duty, but out of a joyful sense of thanksgiving. We become willing to work for justice and equality. We become willing to share freely that which we have, so others may enjoy the sense of fullness and wholeness. We no longer feel that we "should" do anything, because we want to do the work before us. Indeed, we crave opportunities to express our gratitude.

Looking into the sparkling eyes of this faithful woman, I am moved by her selflessness, moved by her joyful witness to the love of God.

———

Willingness must not be confused with readiness insofar as readiness refers to a state of preparedness in relation to certain conditions, a relational state. Also, readiness can be created by external subjects while willingness cannot. I can be well prepared to make a presentation in favor of a parishioner's claim to the magistrate, but remain unwilling to do it. Ma Dludla can be well prepared to tithe, but remain unwilling to do it.

Willingness also must not be confused with motivation, that refers to a state of reaction to stimuli, a causal state. I can be highly motivated to confront the magistrate by the hope of receiving a deserved pension for a parishioner or by the reality of the dire situation I have been asked to represent, yet still remain unwilling to make the presentation. Willingness is a dynamic that empowers readiness and motivation into action.

Willingness remains independent of the conditions in which we find ourselves and the stimuli with which we interact. Willingness can be likened to surrender. When we are willing, we let go of our preconceived notions and expectations and open ourselves to new concepts, new perceptions, and new visions.

Willingness is most often recognized by the physical manifestations that can accompany it, such as the end of a sweat or the cooling of the fevers of defiance and rage. Willingness might be experienced as any of the following:

- the absence of turmoil
- submitting to a force or power greater than personal desire
- relinquishing power
- acceptance
- feeling of empowerment and courage
- open-mindedness, being nonconclusive
- release or absence of physical tension
- serenity, calm, peacefulness (internal acceptance)
- the absence of indecision about the immediate moment; clarity of thought
- the experience of a degree of approval or agreement
- movement away from inaction toward action.

Willingness is an experienced feeling in the Now.

In my own experience, willingness permeates my senses as a physical phenomenon. I experience external changes—for example, clarity in vision: outlines jump into focus, colors become sharp in their contrast. Sometimes sounds enter my consciousness, sounds that may have been present previously but were not heard, had no value or meaning. Sometimes willingness is accompanied by a stretching and a relaxing of muscles throughout my body. A tingling sensation in my arms or legs will cease. My body becomes calm, tranquil. Usually, I also experience internal visual changes: a grey cloud or mist, which has been located behind my eyes and forehead, evaporates. The cloud is a felt presence and becomes a felt absence. Its disintegration can be instantaneous and known immediately, or gradual and perhaps known only in hindsight as much as months or even years later.

There are two levels of willingness, two degrees of a willing experience. On one level, that which is described above, we are willing *with no reservation*. The feeling envelops us and defines our total experience. It is felt as a change, an arrival of something different. There seems to be a physical, an intellectual, and an emotional component in this total experience. Often, an experience of connectedness with a spiritual essence, a higher power, is perceived.

On the other level, one can experience willingness *with reservation*, the degree of reservation varying. A holding back of opinion or agreement accompanies this experience. We may sense willingness physically and intellectually, but not emotionally. Our desire opposes the willing feeling and limits our response to it. This reservation is sensed. It is felt physically, emotionally, and spiritually. The manifestations of this experience of reservation include:

- guilt
- involvement in diversions: sleep, eat, drink, busyness
- feeling uncomfortable about a decision
- obsession about that which we are unwilling to do or face
- captivation by projections that control our consciousness and concern. That which has never existed except as a possibility in our imagination demands and commands our attention.
- physical discomfort: bloated stomach, aching or tingling legs and arms
- sensation of exhaustion: physical or emotional
- indecisiveness

Willingness is not a thing or a substance. It is not an independent entity. It cannot exist by itself the way an organism can. Willingness is dependent upon the individual in which it occurs for being felt, experienced, and acted upon. It is a dynamic attached to a conscious individual. In theological circles this phenomenon of willingness is connected to the power of the Spirit, to God. As Aeschylus wrote, "When a person's willing and eager, God joins in."[3]

Telling the Old, Old Story

"Should I say something?"
"No. He knows what he's saying."
"But, he's wrong. I feel it. He's wrong."
Two voices battle within me.

We sit in the lecture hall, mostly white, middle to upper-middle class Americans.

We have heard a presentation by an African-American woman, a professor at a renowned university. She reminds us white folk that African-American women, people we continue to oppress through our racism, are not going to keep quiet. A "more" famous professor responds articulating his concern that telling her story too many times will turn off her audience. This white man warns this black woman that he is going to get tired of hearing her woes, that there comes a time to stop telling one's story because it has lost its power.

I react with anger. I think, "Look to South Africa to know why a story must be told over and over and over." I know it is not the storyteller's problem in telling too much, but the listener's problem in not truly hearing. It is the persistance of the oppressed, not the compassion or wisdom of the oppressor that tends to be the tool of justice and freedom.

The wisdom of another pastor comes to me, "One is not to congratulate the oppressors for the changes that are happening, but to ask the oppressed what else needs to be changed. Ours is not the posture of neutrality; ours is the posture of integrity, and this gives us different eyes with which to see, [ears with which to hear]—eyes [and ears] that are biased and prejudiced for the people of God."[4]

The group of academicians and theologians blurs into a grey mass. The voice of the person speaking sounds muffled. I feel a flush spread across my neck and up my cheeks.

"Get a hold of yourself," the voice within me commands. "He's the famous professor, remember. You're just a little pastor from a little church in a little state, with little of value to say."

"But, he's wrong. I know it."

"No. If he's wrong, someone else will say something. You'll look like a fool disagreeing with him. He's famous!"

"But, it just isn't right."

"Leave it, Ana."

I want to speak up, but I am unwilling to take the risk. Practicality and appearance win over courage and virtue. "Right, who am I to question his wisdom, anyway—even though I know he's wrong?" I acquiesce. But I retain the right to reconsider, for it does not set right with me.

The famous professor is sitting directly in front of me. I recall a trick I have used many times to help me put things into perspective. I take note that this famous professor wakes up in the morning like the rest of us and goes into the bathroom to urinate. I smile to myself. So, what's the big deal?

My reluctant willingness to remain silent rolls out of me like a wave. A new bold willingness to speak rolls over me. The notion that I should not dispute the famous professor vanishes. Placing my trust in God, I say a prayer for courage as I raise my hand to be recognized.

The two clashing voices within me are silent. I accept that I may be wrong, but I have become willing to take the risk.

The words of an old hymn guide me:

Tell me the old, old story....Tell me the story slowly, that I may take it in....Tell me the story often, for I forget so soon....[5]

"I wish to disagree." My voice is clear and calm. My heart beats quickly out of shyness, but I feel empowered to speak my truth.

I speak of Easter, just past, of the old, old story we must never stop telling, and must seek to hear. I speak of South Africa of the old, old story we must never stop telling, and must seek to hear. I speak of women and blacks in the United States, of the old, old stories we must never stop telling, and must seek to hear.

I see nods. But it does not matter. I will speak my truth and know that I have done right. I am at peace.

At the reception following the presentation and discussion, three women share with me a similar struggle they had endured, being unwilling to disagree aloud with the famous man. Our culture and society cast us in chains, but the power of God can free us. We can become willing to act. Thanks be to God.

> *Let me, O Lord, thy cause defend, a knight without a sword;*
> *No shield I ask, no faithful friend, no vengeance, no reward;*
> *But only in my heart a flame and in my soul a dream,*
> *So that the stones of earthly shame a jeweled crown may seem.[6]*

Each step of a decision or action is in direct relation with a "being willed" phenomenon. While the decision and the action may change, willingness itself remains constant. When making a decision, for example, I can be willing to make the decision to do X; I can be willing to make the decision to *not* do X; I can be willing to do X; or I can be willing to *not* do X. In each case my willingness may or may not be accompanied by a degree of reservation. Consequently, if I make the decision to do X but have reservation, I may remain willing to *not* do X. In other words, after making a decision I may be unwilling to act on it. When I become willing to act on my decision my willingness is in relation to a new decision—the decision to act.

I can stop an action at any time; I can become willing to decide to cease X and then be willing to cease X. These acts of willingness to stop an action do *not* negate the previous experiences of willingness to execute an action.

I am always acting, doing, deciding, and changing. Each act, decision, or change is in relation, to some degree, to my willingness. In the face of reality, my life and experiences continue regardless of my feelings about them. I am always acting out of willingness (conscious or unconscious) to meet reality on some level. Even suicide is in relationship to willingness—willing to be in a new relationship to self and other. Though I cannot determine my future nor change my past (and often not my present, e.g. torture, weather, etc.) my experience of each is one of willingness—willing to accept, willing to reject, willing to be happy, willing to be remorseful.

Willingness is a dynamic component of the Learning Spirit: the willingness to explore and acknowledge truth; the willingness to bracket all of our beliefs in order to consider the possibility of a spiritual power and to experiment with trusting that power; and the willingness to risk, to make mistakes, to act creatively. When we consciously experience this dynamic of willingness within ourselves, the Learning Spirit is engaged and the possibility of genuine learning exists.

Notes

[1]Cited in Hannah Arendt, *Willing: The Life of Mind II* (New York: Harcourt Brace Jovanovich, 1978), 88.

[2]See Alexander Pfänder, *Phenomenology of Willing and Motivation* (Evanston, Illinois: Northwestern University Press, 1967), 21.

[3]Cited in *For Today*, Overeaters Anonymous, 20.

[4]Dr. Albert M. Pennybacker, "On Being Led by a Blind Man," sermon preached at Harvard Avenue Christian Church (Disciples of Christ), Tulsa, Oklahoma, October 27, 1991 (from my notes taken during the sermon).

[5]A. Catherine Hankey, "Tell Me the Old, Old Story," *Wonderful Words of Life* (Carol Stream, Illinois: Hope Publishing Company, 1985), 116.

[6]Jan Struther, "When Stephen, Full of Power and Grace," *Pilgrim Hymnal* (Boston: The Pigrim Press, 1967), 493.

4

THE LEARNING SPIRIT HELIX: TRUTH

"The truth will set you free."
John 8:32b

Touching the Untouchable

The corpse sits balanced atop the wheelbarrow for the five-- kilometer trek to the cemetery. Three people, drenched with sweat, struggle with their load in the summer sun. Stopping the car, Ma Dludla and I climb out to help. We all discuss transporting the body some other way, and settle upon perching the litter on the hood of the car. We load the eldest mourners into the back seat, climb back into the front seat, and drive at a crawl. The Qwabe family walks alongside the car, hands resting on the litter preventing it from falling off and being run over.

The last two kilometers to the cemetery are a cow path winding down a steep hill, unsuitable for the Toyota with its odd load. We leave the car on the road, and five of us, the youngest and the healthiest, hoist the body and start down the hill.

Two hundred meters down the slope, the litter disintegrates in a shower of splinters, bits of twine, and the limp arms and legs of the body. Drenched with sweat and dismay, I stare at the mortal remains of Baba (Mr.) Qwabe: the skin around his ankles peeling away with sores; his stomach caved in; his chest protruding; his fingers like sticks; wrapped only in a ragged sheet and a single blanket. The litter is a loss; we are not moving anybody with that. Each of us takes a corner of the blanket, rolls it in a bit, and we hoist the body again.

Baba Qwabe's head knocks against my knee, and I feel angry. Angry that anyone should be so humiliated even in death...angry at his poverty...angry at the culprits: apartheid, racism, and greed. Here with Baba Qwabe against my knee, apartheid is so real, not an abstract system, but something concrete and repulsive.

One of the women carrying Baba Qwabe collapses from the heat. There she is on the ground with the body lying on top of her. Someone runs off to fetch water for her, and the rest of us pick up the body for the final kilometer to the grave.

At the graveside, I read the service. At the time to lower the body into the hole, only four of us feel up to the task, so I climb in with Baba Qwabe's son. The women hand us Baba Qwabe's sleeping mat to be spread on the floor of the grave. His bed in life will be his bed in death. His mat, completely stained and soaked with urine, is a mute but smelly testimony to the sort of existence Baba Qwabe has led in the last months of his life, bedridden and cared for by people too poor and too broken to improve his lot.

The body is lowered. Gently we lay him to rest. A final indignity: he doesn't quite fit. We curl his legs under him, cover him with the blanket, then place a second mat on top. We climb out.

I close the service. It is time to close the grave. The four of us who have not yet succumbed to the heat grab the shovels, pick, and hoe and scoop the soil into the grave. Forty-five minutes finishes the job; Baba Qwabe is buried.

Ma Dludla and I leave the family, return to the car, and drive home....

As I read this macabre tale Tod has recalled, I am horrified into a bitter laughter with tears. I am continually horrified by tragedies such as this life and death of Baba Qwabe...tragedies explained away by most white South Africans:

- *He was probably a drunk.*
- *"They" all drink.*
- *"They" are such dirty people.*
- *"They" must be happy to live the way they do or "they" would try to change it.*
- *There is plenty of work; "they" are just lazy.*
- *"They" do not respect their elders.*
- *"They" do not wash.*

The sense of these sharp comments is, "Don't touch; it (i.e., disease, poverty, dirt, hard luck) might rub off." In effect these racist and classist slurs, these lies and myths, justify the oppressive status quo. They work together to create and maintain a social class of untouchables, to create and maintain fear of the poor. These sentiments are upheld and promoted by both the South African and the international press.

The truth of poverty is knowable. Poverty, like death, is confrontational when we allow ourselves to get near it. It is hard and repugnant, and is especially abhorrent and frightening to those who have not touched it, or have not been touched by it. There is something about touching or experiencing poverty and apartheid on a personal level that moves us more than pictures or statistics ever can. Poverty is the result of those who, like myself, have resources and do not share them. Poverty is a cycle from which it can be extremely difficult, if not impossible, to free oneself, but usually not because of any innate fault of the poor person.

The truth about apartheid is knowable and is manifested in this life—the life and death of Baba Qwabe. Truly, we need courage from God to stand on the side of truth.

Truth is one of the three strands of the helix of the Learning Spirit. As we attempt to understand the essence and experience of truth, we must bear in mind at all times this helix in which truth is experienced and known, and its interrelatedness to willingness, trust, and creative action.

Truth is a process of knowing and participating in that knowledge. When we attempt to control truth, to conceal it or warp it, we are effectively suppressing the process of truth. When we institute myths and lies, and ban participation in genuine truth, we are attempting to thwart the power of truth to engage others in the Learning Spirit. But, as history points out, such attempts to suppress truth and its spokespeople cannot suppress the power of the Learning Spirit. Such attempts can only create foils and barriers. Truth inevitably re-emerges, often to the detriment of those who have tried to suppress and bury it.

Silenced

With excitement and anticipation we stand at the arrival hall of Durban's Louis Botha Airport. I am filled with that feeling of emotional energy that comes when waiting for family one has not seen in a long time.

The passengers from Johannesburg's shuttle flight begin surging through the doors. To my surprise, the first person I recognize disembarking is not my Aunt Helen, whom we are expecting, but our good friend, Barbara, who had taught with us at Inanda High School during our first year in South Africa.

I take Barbara into my arms with a warm hug, and she bursts out crying, "I've lost them both...." Her sobs consume her.

I notice the black mourning patch pinned to her blouse.

"They killed them both, knocked at the front door," she speaks between sobs. "They had practiced getting out the back if this happened. They went into the yard, but the house was surrounded. They didn't even try to arrest them. They just shot them down...," her voice trails off.

"Who, Barb? Who was shot down?" I ask softly.

"My parents," comes the muffled reply.

I recall the newspaper article earlier in the week: "Dr. and wife killed in Mamelodi." I had not realized they were Barbara's parents.

Who were Barbara's parents?

Who were Florence and Fabian Ribeiro?

They were ordinary people...professionals. A doctor. A social worker. Black South Africans. Residing in Mamelodi, a township of Pretoria. Ordinary people who lived with phone threats, bomb blasts on their home, constant observance by the Secret Police, escape plans. Ordinary people shot down when they fled, clad in nightclothes, out their back door into the spotlights and guns of their assassins. Ordinary people trying to be faithful to a God of truth and life in this trying time in the history of their people.

Why the Ribeiro's? Why were they blacklisted and marked for assassination? Terrorists? So the media would have us believe. Troublemakers? So the government was convinced.

They were ordinary people....Fabian doctored many people, often the poor, and most recently those injured in the township "skirmishes" with the South African Police and military forces—those gassed, burned, beaten, and shot by the "occupying" forces. His patients, old and young, were doing everyday things from playing in backyards to attending school, to mourning the dead.

Ordinary people...Florence (unlike Mrs. Zwane serving the white Magistrate in Melmoth) concerned herself with advocacy for welfare cases, trying to secure pensions and health care for people who qualify but can't quite leap the numerous hurdles of apartheid's red tape.

Ordinary people...but Fabian and Florence Ribeiro ignored laws that impose silence on the township violence and massacres. They opposed the suppression of truth. They consistently reported to their church and its ecumenical connections the suffering of their patients and clients and the injustices they witnessed. They had been warned by many to keep their mouths shut. They risked and have finally given their lives in the belief that people around the country and around the world must know that all is not well in South Africa, contrary to what the South African government would have us all believe.

Ordinary people...with an extraordinary faith, a faith that directed their work and made them witnesses of God's love unto death.

"They killed them both," Barbara whispers.

Barbara's husband arrives to greet her. They drift away, Barbara like a tiny bundle under her husband's broad arm.

That evening we read a small article reporting that a neighbor of the Ribeiros recorded the license number of the car in which the killers fled. The vehicle has been traced to the South African Police Department's motor pool. The police have denied any involvement in the incident.

It was now about the sixth hour, and darkness came over the whole land until the ninth hour, for the sun stopped shining. And the curtain of the temple was torn in two.

Luke 23:44–45

People ask us, pleading for soft lies, "Are things in South Africa as bad as the media reports?" They hope for the false security of reassuring myths. They yearn to hear of other families in South Africa who are not *marked for assassination and continue more normal lives. They want to accept a reasonable explanation for the Ribeiros' murders. They do not want to hear of the possibility of a government plot. They do not want to be reminded that people doing good can be shot and killed. They do not want to hear of the orphans left behind. They exemplify the words of T.S. Eliot, "Human kind cannot bear very much reality."* [1]

The Ribeiros' murders were filed as unsolved cases for more than three years. Now a new government has come into power, and talk of the horrors of the past regime is ripe. Old myths and lies are revealed. The Natal Mercury newspaper reported in July 1990:

RIBEIRO KILLINGS;
FORMER SELOUS SCOUT NAMED

A former Selous Scout is to be questioned in connection with the December 1986 murders of Mamelodi doctor Fabian Ribeiro and his wife Florence.

Judge Louis Harms will also decide this week whether startling new evidence implicating members of the now disbanded Civil Co-operation Bureau in the killings is to be dealt with....The new evidence came to light just twenty-

*four hours after retiring Defence Force chief General
Jannie Geldenhuys announced that the CCB had been disbanded.*[2]

Those who hold power can manipulate and control truth for
either an individual or a group of people by controlling and limiting access to information and to experiences. Lies can be enforced
and myths propagated. When alternative and often contradicting
"truths" are set before us, it can be difficult to judge and finally
choose among them.

We tend to determine what is true by considering which "truth"
best serves us. What is accepted as true is what we want to be true.

As George Orwell describes in his book *1984*, truth can be,
and often is, blatantly filtered and changed by a government or
power group. Under apartheid, the South African government actively attempted to determine truth for its people. This was apparent in the myths about poverty espoused by the ruling class of South
Africa, in the case of the Ribeiros' murders, and in the suppression
of communism and anything considered subversive. More recently,
a myth upheld as truth was created in the portrayal of the enmity
between Inkatha and the African National Congress. The tension
between the two groups was described not as a political reality and
a direct result of the racial oppression of apartheid, but rather as an
aspect of the so-called volatile nature of black Africans. In this
case as in others, the white government established a self-serving
myth and promoted it as truth through the media, especially televi-
sion.

Not surprisingly, the South African Broadcasting Corporation,
responsible for extensive propogation of the myths of apartheid, is
operated and financed as a governmental department. Airwaves
are owned and controlled by the government. Under apartheid, the
members of the controlling board were appointed by the white State
President, and the board reported to the white Minister of Foreign
Affairs and Information.

"They make ready their tongue like a bow, to shoot lies; it is not by truth that they triumph in the land."

Jeremiah 9:3a

Another means by which South Africa has attempted to control truth is through the manipulation of theology. The "state theology" in South Africa provided the theological justification for the racism and oppression of apartheid.[3] Theological concepts and biblical texts were misused to promote obedience to and trust in the state itself. Under apartheid, the state was portrayed as the incarnation of truth and goodness. Theology became defined by the state to fit its own needs.

Vital theology can never allow itself to be above suspicion and examination. Vital theology is always a process of discovery and revelation, engaged in by a theologian or any person of faith. Theologizing is an ongoing undertaking. Yet the South African apartheid state made use of a tightly controlled interpretation of Christian theology to justify its oppressive tactics. Tragically, millions of people were, and many still are, fooled and confused by false theological proclamations.

Accept Thy Lot

Died: 9 April 1986, nine months old
Themba (Hope) Ntuli
- *a son of a son*
- *the Ntuli future*

Born: July 1985
Home: Matshana Black Spot
- *no fresh water*
- *no electricity*
- *no plumbing or sewage*
- *dirt roads*
- *overcrowded*
- *five kilometers from Empangeni,*
  a prosperous whites-only town

Father: employed by the South African police force
- *stationed in Transvaal 350 kilometers away*
- *last home in January*

Mother: employed in Durban, 200 kilometers away
- *last home 29 March to bring money on her regular month-end visit*

Funeral: 12 April, 10:00 a.m.

Themba's coffin, draped by a soft blanket, is bedecked with a small plastic dome full of plastic flowers. We women have gathered in the narrow room to share in his mother's grief. She sits, her face shrouded by a blanket, still. A few latecomers ask to view Themba's tiny head, serenely shrouded in white ruffles, to say a last good-bye. Coins clink in the dish beside the ever-burning candle. A dirge rises in the stillness. Like echoes, we join in the chant muffled by the heavy rain on the metal roof. A prayer. A blessing. Communion. Remember, "God is with us."

We process singing, over rain-filled ruts of a road, behind the pick-up truck bearing Themba to the cemetery beside the Lutheran church. Grandfather, walking with us through this barren land, comments, "We are lucky to have had this site allocated when they used to give land to the churches. Now they give nothing." Is it anger or despair that I hear in his voice?

The men have dug and prepared the tiny, unwelcome grave. Now they wait, drenched and muddy, shovels and picks in hand. Grandmother, with tears in her eyes, whispers, "My son has arrived in time to say good-bye to his son." The tiny casket is opened one last time, for a final meeting of father and son, two strangers.

Rows of tiny graves surround this new one. Some are marked with wooden crosses, some with a single stick, others recognizable only by the settling mounds. Some are named. Most are nameless. On Themba's left: Sibongile (We have given thanks) Ngubana, five months. On Themba's right: Nomusa (Mercy) Mbuli, nine months. South Africa's children. South Africa's future.

Death of children has been much a stranger to me. In my thirty years, I have known only two American children who have died.

Here in South Africa, in one year, I have buried four children. Causes of death: measles, asthma, and malnutrition. Reason for death: black in South Africa.

Familiar phrases have other meanings here.

"God gives and God takes away." We are deceiving ourselves if we defend this situation as God's intervention in the lives of these children. God takes away in old age. Nature takes away by catastrophe or incurable illness. But measles, asthma, and malnutrition—humans are causing these deaths.

> *GOD does NOT keep people hungry.*
> *GOD does NOT take parents away.*
> *GOD does NOT insist on pit toilets or no toilets.*
> *GOD does NOT make fresh and clean water a luxury.*
> *GOD does NOT profit from food sales to the poor.*
> *GOD does NOT covet medical care for a chosen few.*
> *GOD does NOT favor people-without-color.*

"God gives each according to her/his need." Here, what God has given to meet basic needs is taken away by others. God has not created a world in which cups emptied by greed are divinely re-filled.

"Accept thy lot" is a biblical message often given to black South Africans by those in power. But what does it mean? What did it mean for Themba? For his parents? Is the "lot" of twenty-eight million Africans-of-color to be victimized by a six million white minority, or is it their lot and our lot to recognize truth and work for change?

"Give to Caesar what is Caesar's" (Luke 20:25b). In South Africa, what does God call Themba's family and all other black African families to render to the white National Party Government? Their children's lives? Their family life? Their homes? Their education? Their nationality and citizenship? Their dignity?

...Themba's grave is filled. The spot for the next grave is clearly marked. Ready. Waiting.

Twenty-eight months ago, I arrived in South Africa. I believed then that apartheid was wrong. But I had no understanding of the complex system of myths that uphold it. Watching Themba's tiny casket lowered into the earthen grave, watching the grave fill shovel by shovel, I sense for the first time the true depths of the horror of the apartheid reality.

How do we know what truth is?

There is no set formula for testing truth. While we can uphold truth as an ultimate and unchanging reality, the specifics surrounding any event or idea do change. Therefore, any testing of truth is necessarily situational. Truth submerges itself in paradoxes, always defying our imposed logical and scientific systems.

We can know truth only from the inside out, only from being a living part of it, only by participating in it.[4] It is the moment in which we find ourselves, the NOW, that holds truth.

Vision in the Now

This academician beside me is an enigma. His vision is clear, yet he is an underdog in the academic world, a thorn in its side because he will not adapt. He will not "write his papers for the professors." His vision drives him and empowers him. I ask myself, "Is he a failure or a success?" I convince myself he is a failure, telling myself he could have a "good" teaching job if he wanted it.

Together we are at a workshop investigating mandatory education and voluntary education. The discussions begin to pierce my dark lenses and the myths I hold true about academia. I begin to ask myself questions about my own learning and education:

- *So I have degrees—what have I learned?*
- *So I have passed exams—how have the courses affected my life?*
- *Have I just been accumulating knowledge in order to participate in academic discourse?*

- *For whom have I written all these papers and exams? For the professors or for myself?*
- *Have I been seeking certification or wisdom?*

I begin to contemplate the possibility of taking control of my own learning. I wonder if I have ever been a voluntary learner in an academic setting? Dare I risk taking the control of my learning out of the hands of the professors who hold the power of naming me a failure or a success through the grading process, and for whom a twenty-page term paper is always a twenty-page term paper? Dare I risk taking the control of my learning out of the hands of the institution that holds the power to grant or withhold a degree?

Something clicks for me.[5]

After being confronted by the truth about myself and my own learning and schooling, I make some decisions about my education that change the direction of my life. I realize that my confrontations with truth will usually occur outside of and in spite of the schooling environments professional educators create. On the other hand, I learn that schooling sometimes provides opportunities to experience and to learn truth, opportunities to deduce, to question, to analyze, to decipher, to internalize truth.

I am free to choose. No longer does the academic degree hold its primacy. No longer is the professor an expert to fear and to blindly obey. I begin making choices to claim my education for myself, and, in many cases, to opt out of traditional schooling.

During the next two years, as my vision clears and my own darkness recedes, I begin to recognize the success enjoyed by that academic underdog. He has chosen to put his trust in truth and to act creatively in response to truth. To act faithfully, he has been willing to risk everything including a prestigious job in academia and the financial remuneration that goes with it. He can freely advocate bold alternatives to co-option and darkness and provide to others a vision in the Now.

Truth is often equated to light and sight: the light that enables us to see, and the sight we have in that light. In his letter to the early Christians at Corinth, Paul writes, "For God...made God's light shine in our hearts to give us the light of the knowledge of the glory of God..." (2 Corinthians 4:6). Truth illuminates both mind and heart, and is illuminated, becoming visible and knowable to both mind and heart.

Truth opposes lies upheld by deception, dishonesty, and myths. Truth is the liberating knowledge about our environment that frees us to act creatively in that environment. The command of the oracle at Delphi, "Know thyself," is a call to truth, to illumination of ourselves and our environment, a call to become fully educated and fully human.

A central paradox of truth is that once defined, truth remains open to further examination and redefinition. While we can uphold an ultimate truth, we must remain open to new revelations of truth, or the rigidity of our stance will put into question the ultimacy of that truth we expound. Truth teaches us and engages us in a process. It can neither limit us nor close our minds for then it loses its power as the truth that will set us free.

The ability to determine and prove truth does not lie in the realm of science. Truth cannot be computed by any formula. Its existence is determined by experience: the experience of an individual in a community. The proof of truth lies in the affirmations of those who discover it and uphold it. The different voices of community are treasures when truth is sought. Each voice must be heard, weighed, and tested. While some voices will clang with untruth, others will join together to reveal the fullness of truth.

What Price Freedom?

Once to every heart and nation comes the moment to decide,
In the strife of truth with falsehood, for the good or evil side.

*Some great cause, God's new messiah, offering each the
    bloom or blight.*
*And the choice goes by forever twixt that darkness and
    that light.*[6]

"*Ma, look! Nelson Mandela's going to be released today.*"
"What?" cries my companion, Ma Dludla. "Give me that paper."

*The few people in the shop where we have stopped early on
this Sunday morning turn their heads sharply at Ma Dludla's outburst. She reads the column quickly, joy spreading across her face,
her eyes twinkling with tears.*

*The rest of our journey to Ngcaka (en-na-ga) is filled with our
giddy joy. A large Mercedes driven by a white couple speeds past,
raising a cloud of dust and a shower of small stones. "They're on
their way to Cape Town to welcome Nelson Mandela from prison,"
jokes Ma Dludla with a laugh. I think to myself how unlikely this is,
for the whites in this region of northern Natal are notoriously conservative, and Cape Town is more than 2,000 kilometers distant!*

*The joy of Mandela's release and our trip to the congregation
at Ngcaka will always be an intoxicating memory for me.*

*A month later, Ma Dludla and I head for Ngcaka again, and I
am suffused with the memory of that joyful feeling from our previous trip. But my euphoria drains away as we near our destination,
and I am pulled back into the reality of my parishioners here in
this remote place.*

*On the nearest hillside, the home of Baba Moses Mdlalose, a
deacon of the church, looks forlorn. The yard stands empty of cows
and goats. The thatched roof of one hut sags, while others are gone
completely, like their inhabitants. The harsh restrictions enforced
by Mr. Smuts, the white farmer and legal owner of this land,
prompted Moses to flee, like his namesake, but there is no promised land on which Moses Mdlalose can settle.*

*We are greeted by three deacons whose faces tell us of trouble.
Baba Mbuli, a man about forty years old, looks especially haggard
with his drawn face, sunken eyes, and gapped-tooth grimace.*

Baba Zwane begins (in Zulu). "After our meeting with Chief Nkosi and Magistrate Badenhorst which you'd arranged, Umfundisi (Pastor), it looked as though the government would prevent the white farmers from restricting the numbers of our cattle, goats and horses, or from making us pay a fee to keep them. Things seemed good. But things have gone from bad to worse. Baba Hadebe was told to relocate like Baba Mdlalose and the others who have left. Last week, when he refused to go, the white farmers came and burned his kraal to force him off the land. Things here never change."

"Did you report this to the police?" asks Ma Dludla.

"The police!? The police led the farmers to Baba Hadebe's home and helped them burn it," Baba Mgomezulu's voice is tired.

I run the problem through my head. Our parishioners and their ancestors have lived on this land for generations. In the 1880s the land was "legally" deeded to the whites by other whites. The original black African farmers then became the laborers on the large land tracts held by the new white farmers. Now the black African labor force has multiplied along with the livestock they need to survive. The white farmers with mechanization do not need as many workers and want more acreage for planting and grazing. In an effort to drive people away, the white farmers have commenced charging black African families for the animals they keep, animals essential for their survival: five rands ($2) per month for each cow, maximum six cows; ten rands ($4) per month per horse, maximum one horse. These fees are reminiscent of the 1918 hut tax. Is it mere coincidence that the forty rands total equals exactly each worker's average monthly wage?

Some of the workers have fled, like our deacon, Moses Mdlalose, now trying to make it in a township. Some have been burned out like Baba Hadebe. Some are staying and wasting away like Baba Mbuli.

Yes, we had alerted the authorities, the area's chief and the magistrate, a year ago. Yes, there had been hope. But now that hope is in ashes like Baba Hadebe's home. It seems that things here will never change.

Time for church. We open with a hymn. The Zulu words rise majestically:

> *By the light of burning martyrs, Jesus' bleeding feet I track.*
> *Toiling up new Calvaries ever with the cross that turns not*
>   *back.*
> *New occasions teach new duties, time makes ancient good*
>   *uncouth.*
> *They must upward still and onward, who would keep*
>   *abreast of truth.*[7]

There are those in South Africa who are learning that "time makes ancient good uncouth." White colonialism, imperialism, paternalism, apartheid are giving way. Yet others are angry that their way of life, legitimized and protected by that same racism and apartheid, is threatened by the uncovering of truth. Fearful, they are torching Baba Hadebe's kraal less than one month after Mandela's release. They are determined to keep things the way they have always been.

This large round hut, Baba Mbuli's home, holds nearly one hundred of us gathered for worship. We sit on grass mats atop a dung floor. My eyes scan the faces of the congregation:

* *filled with pain, yet knowing hope.*
* *surrounded by evil, yet knowing that God wants good.*
* *living in fear; yet knowing strength in faith.*
* *facing defeat, yet ever accepting new challenges of the cross.*
* *constantly pushed back by the "boss" and the society, yet always toiling upwards and onwards.*

> *Though the cause of evil prosper, yet tis truth alone is*
>   *strong.*
> *Truth forever on the scaffold, wrong forever on the throne.*
> *Yet that scaffold sways the future, and behind the dim*
>   *unknown*
> *Standeth God within the shadow keeping watch above*
>   *God's own.*[8]

Truth can be exciting for one and alarming for another. Good news for some is often bad news for others. Those in power may try to suppress truth until it becomes too powerful an opponent. They may shroud themselves in familiar clichés, seeking reminders of the "way things were" and hoping beyond hope that things will never change.

Apartheid was enforced not only by myths, propaganda, and social custom, but by national legislation. In 1948, the white electorate of South Africa voted into power the National Party government, whose policy until mid-1991 was apartheid. In short, the Nationalist Party government believed racial and ethnic groups must be kept apart, and resources must be divided as the white government saw fit.

Legally, apartheid was upheld by more than three hundred laws dealing with racial separation and control. While the laws were based upon race, ethnicity, and color, they were largely motivated by economics and greed.

Some Will Make You Laugh; Some Will Make You Cry

It is our first morning in South Africa. We take advantage of the time change to enjoy an early morning stroll. We practice our Zulu by greeting each person we meet. We are surprised at the number of people already out at 4:30 a.m.

At each corner two or three black African men wait. Like shadows, they board buses that seem to slide almost silently through these suburban streets.

At breakfast our white host patiently listens to our questions. "Where do the black men live? Isn't this a "whites-only" neighborhood? Where are the buses taking them? Do they come every morning? Who are they?"

The answers: These men live with their wives, who are domestic servants. The law says the husbands can not live in the maids' quarters. The law says the husband must live in the black township or in the black Homeland. They stay in the white suburb illegally.

The whites know they stay. The government knows they stay. The men work in the city. They need to get to work. The stores and businesses need them to arrive on time. The townships and home-lands are far from the city. The government provides the buses to take them to and from work.

"But if it's illegal?" I query. "I thought the whole point of apartheid is to keep whites and blacks separate!"

Our host explains how the system works to meet the supply and demand needs of labor. It also works to keep whites and blacks quiet, for, as in this case, both whites and blacks are engaged in illegal activity and can be arrested at any time.

The truth about apartheid is well masked.

"When you tell them all this, they will not listen to you....Truth has perished; it has vanished from their lips."
Jeremiah 7:28

Becoming familiar with the specific laws of apartheid and how they are (or are not) enforced demonstrates the extent to which the lives of South African citizens are controlled by the State, and the levels of deception used to enforce this control. Some laws will make you laugh. Some will make you cry.

Three legal pillars—the Mixed Marriage Act, the Population Registration Act, and the Group Areas Act—upheld apartheid.[9]

The Prohibition of Mixed Marriage Act *(No. 55) of 1949 prohibited marriages between black Africans and whites and was amended to cover all interracial marriages between members of any of the four population groups classified in Act No. 30 of 1950. The Immorality Act (No. 5) of 1927 had set the foundation for the Mixed Marriage Act by prohibiting "illicit" sexual intercourse be-tween whites and black Africans and stipulated a five-year jail sen-tence for infractions. In 1950 this was amended to make all sexual relations between a black African and a white criminal offenses, and was extended to criminalize sexual relations across all color-lines. The Mixed Marriage Act was removed as law in 1986.*

The Population Registration Act *(No. 30) of 1950 created a new population group designation, so-called coloreds, resulting in four population groups: European (white), so-called colored (people of mixed heritage), Asian (descendants of indentured servants brought in the 1860's from India), and Bantu (black African). This act established the means of identifying and controlling population groups.*

The Group Areas Act *(No. 51) of 1950 set forth the legal designation and separation of land for each population group. This act was preceded by the Native Land Act of 1913, which prohibited the purchase of land outside designated reserves (later called homelands) by black Africans, and the Natives Act of 1923 (commonly known as the Urban Areas Act), which segregated urban communities and was amended in 1945 to forbid any black African from remaining in an urban area for more than seventy-two hours without a permit.*

The enforcement of these racial zoning acts led to the enactment of the Natives Resettlement Act (No. 19) of 1954, which resulted in the expropriation of property and the forced removal of more than two million people (1.5 million of whom were black Africans) by 1976 and tens of thousands since then. All Group Area legislation was consolidated in the Group Areas Act (No. 77) of 1957.

While these three "pillars of apartheid" kept everyone in line, the details of the apartheid legal machine continued to be worked out. As unexpected situations arose in the society, white privilege was protected through the creation and ratification of new laws. A selection of such laws is listed below.

1. **The Bantu Authorities Act** *of 1951 established Bantustans (reservations) for the separate development of black Africans. This act reserved 87 percent of the country's land for white use only. All people of color, 70 percent of the South African population, were relegated to the remaining 13 percent of the land area. Bantustans were preceded by "reserves" officially demarcated in 1913 and 1936. In 1972 the term "homeland" replaced*

Bantustan. The homelands divided black Africans on tribal lines, created "black states," and forced all black South Africans to lose their citizenship in the Republic.

Ten homelands were envisioned. Seven were established: Transkei, Ciskei, KwaZulu, Gazankulu, Venda, Bophuthatswana, and Qwa Qwa. These are all overcrowded and economically depressed areas.

2. **The Pass Law** *of 1952, in an attempt to maintain control and order through influx control, required that every black African be fingerprinted and carry a passbook (i.e. reference and documentation book). The penalty for not carrying the passbook was initially fifty pounds sterling or six months in jail, but the sentence was reduced as fines could not be collected from the poor and jails filled with the hundreds of thousands of black Africans arrested under this law.*

3. **Job Reservation** *was controlled by a series of acts that created jobs and job opportunities for whites by taking the jobs and opportunities away from people of color. These acts included:*

   A. **The Mines and Work Act** *(No. 12) of 1911, known as the "Colour Bar Act," excluded black Africans from being eligible to receive certificates of competence, thereby closing off upgrading potential.*

   B. **The Apprenticeship Act** *of 1922 closed off possibilities for black African advancement by restricting apprenticeship programs to whites.*

   C. **The Industrial Conciliation Act** *of 1956 institutionalized job reservation by designating job qualification according to population group and excluding black Africans from recognized trade unions. In 1970 an amendment empowered the Minister of Bantu Administration to prohibit the employment of black Africans in any specified area, trade, or job. For example, in 1970, this law was used to prohibit the employment of black Africans as counter attendants,* *or cashiers in stores, or as receptionists, typists, or telephone operators in offices, factories, and hotels.*[10]

D. The Wage Acts *of 1925 and 1957 nationalized maximum wages payable to members of each population group.*

E. The Nursing Act *(No. 69) of 1957 stipulated that a "nonwhite" nurse could not supervise a white nurse.*

4. The Reservation of Separate Amenities Act *of 1953 established the legal designation of all "public" facilities for use by specific population groups without the development of equal facilities for all population groups. An amendment in 1960 reserved sea bathing areas for whites only. (This act was removed as law on 2 February, 1990.)*

5. The Bantu Education Act *(No. 47) of 1953 nationalized education for black Africans and declared private schools for black Africans illegal. This forced the closure of numerous church-operated schools that refused to register as state schools and thereby come under the authority of the state and the state prescribed curriculum. This also ensured that white children attended the best schools, and black African children were educated for a low place in society. This act also restricted the location of educational programs for black Africans, making it illegal for a black African to participate in functions held in white areas; for example, it was illegal for a black African to attend an educational class or Bible study held at a church in a white area.*

6. The Extension of University Education Act *(No. 45) of 1959 excluded black Africans from all existing institutions of higher education and established separate colleges and universities for black Africans, so-called coloreds and Indian Africans.*

7. The National Education Policy Act *of 1967 stipulated that schooling for whites was to be free, including books and stationery, while black Africans would continue to pay fees. Ac-*

cording to a study undertaken by the Universities of Natal and Cape Town, "In 1986 the government spent 2,508 rands [approximately $1,003] on the schooling of every white child, half that (1,094 rands and 1,021 rands) [approximately $440 and $408] on Indian [African] and [so-called] colored school students, and less than a quarter of that (477 rands) [approximately $190] on every [black] African child."[11]

The mindset behind the execution of these education acts is illustrated in the following statement made in 1953 by Dr. Hendrik Verwoerd, then Minister of Native Affairs and later Prime Minister, "If the native in South Africa today...is taught to expect that they will live their adult life under a policy of equal rights they are making a big mistake....There is no place for them in the European community above the level of certain forms of labour...."[12]

8. **Tri-Parliamentary Representation** *maintained power for the whites, introduced freedom of political participation (without power) for so-called coloreds and Indian Africans, and completely excluded political participation of black Africans, the majority of the country's population.*

9. **The Internal Security Act** *of 1976 consolidated several preceding acts that had prohibited free speech and expression through censorship and banning of individuals, organizations, and publications. Banning is the legal restriction of speech, movement, and activity. Some of these included:*
   A. *Act No. 38 of 1927 made it possible to ban an individual without a trial.*
   B. The Suppression of Communism Act *(No. 44) of 1950 declared the Communist party illegal and criminalized anyone encouraging or defending any related form of that doctrine. This act criminalized spokespeople in the church, in labor, and in other anti-apartheid groups. The oppressive use of this act is described by a group of eminent South African church people and theologians who gathered in*

1986 and wrote The Kairos Document. *They write, "Anything that threatens the status quo is labelled 'communist'. Anyone who opposes the State and especially anyone who rejects its theology is simply dismissed as a 'communist'. No account is taken of what communism really means....The state uses the label 'communist' in an uncritical and unexamined way as its symbol of evil."*[13]

C. The Criminal Law Amendment *was passed in reaction to an African National Congress protest at which eight thousand people were jailed. This act made passive resistance a crime.*

D. The Riotous Assemblies Act *of 1956 authorized magistrates to prohibit any public gathering of twelve or more people; it was amended in 1974 to cover gatherings of any size.*

E. The Unlawful Organizations Act *(No. 34) of 1960 banned the African National Congress and the Pan African Congress, among other anti-apartheid groups.*

F. The Departures from the Union Regulation Act *(No. 34) of 1955 could be enforced to deprive citizens of the Republic and the Bantustans the right to travel abroad.*

G. The Customs Act *(No. 55) of 1955 created categories of goods and literature that could be prohibited from importation. Section 21 of the act included the children's storybook* Black Beauty.

H. Banning Orders *empowered the Minister of Justice to place a banning order on any person or organization considered to be engaged in activities that endangered or were calculated to endanger the security of the state or the maintenance of public order. Banning orders restricting speech, movement, and activity were applied to black consciousness and anti-apartheid movements and spokespersons.*

I. The Terrorism Act *criminalized any act that in the eyes of the government, increased hostility between the whites and other inhabitants of the Republic.*

Together in our host's kitchen we have laughed at some of the more ludicrous apartheid laws. Yet tears sting my eyes as the horror of apartheid begins to take shape in my mind. These laughable laws have destroyed families, homes, churches, and communities. For many South Africans tears are all that they have left.

———

Our ability to recognize truth is limited in many ways. We have been socialized into certain cultural ideologies and belief systems that bind us like steel wires. "They are the bones and sinews of a society's culture. They reproduce themselves in the children born into and brought up in it, socialized and inculturated into it. They provide the community context within which people see, perceive, understand, relate, and reject, work and relax, love and hate."[14]

Archbishop Denis Hurley grew up sheltered and isolated in white South Africa. He did not question the way things were. He did not see things differently, so went along with the status quo.

As a young Catholic seminarian, he traveled to Rome to attend the Oblate Scholasticate, where he worshiped, studied, and mingled with many people of color from around the world. This interaction confronted Hurley's understanding of truth and jolted his reality. He managed to step out of the tangle of social steel wires that ensnared him. He discovered that skin color does not immediately entitle one to a superior social status, nor does it necessarily relegate one to an inferior social status. In his own words, "I saw [for the first time] that the South African treatment of black people was an offence against human dignity and freedom and from then on this conviction was working subconsciously on me."[15]

Unfortunately, for most white South Africans, this confrontation with truth about human dignity and freedom is not part of their experience.

One Big Happy Family

*If anyone has material possessions and sees his brother in
need and has not pity on him, how can the love of God be
in him? Dear children, let us not love with words or tongue
but with actions and in truth. This then is how we know
that we belong to the truth....*

1 John 3:17–19a

"*I just can't afford to pay her more. And she's absolutely indispensable. Besides she's been with us for eight years. I got her from
the woman who used to live in our home before us. I couldn't just
throw her out on the street! Besides, the children love her. She's
like one of the family.*" *Mrs. Botha's face glows pink in the soft
candlelight. The mauve walls cushion us together as we sit sated
by the feast of ham shanks and yams.*

*Our host, John, calls again for the servant, "Florence, clear
the table, please."*

Tod and I rise to help, as we would as guests at any home.

"*No, no! Sit,*" *John waves us back to our seats. "Florence will
do that. That's why she's here."*

*We carry out our dishes in spite of John's protests, placing
them on the counter, thanking Mrs. Mpungose for the tasty dinner
she has prepared but has not eaten. I wonder if John or Mrs. Botha
know Florence's last name.*

*Mrs. Mpungose looks tired. After all she has been up and "on
duty" since morning tea, fourteen hours earlier.*

"*She's such a hard worker. We can't complain,*" *Mrs. Botha's
words welcome us back into the dining room. "And I do pay her a
decent wage, more than my neighbor pays hers. I'm just sorry I
can't afford to pay her more."*

*Our conversation drifts away from Florence Mpungose, the
ever-present nonmember of the Botha family. She quietly finishes
clearing the platters from the sideboard, and the conversation turns
to horses. Mr. and Mrs. Botha begin to share their anxieties over
an upcoming horse show in which they are entering five of their
horses.*

*"I can't afford to pay her more," really means, "I don't want
to pay her more. I will use my money for other things, like my
horses." The job remains the same, long hours six days per week,
regardless of the salary. There is no consideration that the money
available might determine the hours to be worked.*

*"I give her perks. I pay her children's school fees. I buy her
uniforms." These perks only increase the dependency of the worker
on the "Madam," the white employer. And the "Madam" gets to
bask in her seeming generosity.*

*So often we enjoy our security and comforts by justifying our-
selves with lies and myths.*

We are limited not only by our social attitudes but also by our
senses, our language, and our physical body. We are limited by our
need to be accepted within our community, our church, our ethnic
group, our family. We are limited by the rules of science that select
and categorize truth for us. In South Africa, people are limited by
their schooling and so-called education.

He Deserves a Chance

Mid-December in rural Mfanefile...

*I stand in silence, surveying the tragic sight. Glimmering sheets
of iron roofing now twisted and crumpled, steam from the heat of
the early morning sun. As if some giant's hand had ripped them off
and balled them up like discarded tinfoil, they now lie scattered
across the weedy knoll.*

*The rafters, snapped by the previous night's windstorm, jut
skyward like the ribs of a dead animal's skeleton. The gutters hang
from their brackets askew like limp limbs, and the classroom floors
are awash with rain water.*

*Cebisa Secondary School, completed only two weeks ago, is in
shambles. Our hopes of higher education for our community lie
crumpled and steaming, the work of a single storm. My shoulders*

droop, not so much from the weight of my baby in his backpack, as from the sense of defeat I feel.

Early January in Edendale, a township...

The thumping of the police helicopter overhead reduces our conversation to a whisper as if the police might overhear what we say.

"Edendale is a war zone and has been for nearly a year now," says Mr. Dube in a hushed tone. "More than three hundred have been killed in the last ten months, and we're going to another funeral this Saturday."

"We've decided to send Bonga away for school this year. He's twelve now. He deserves a chance. There is no learning in these schools here. Political groups are recruiting in the classrooms. The teachers are afraid of the students. It's chaos!"

We recall the graffiti splashed on a classroom wall, "When the going gets tough, the teacher gets going."

Mr. Dube explodes, "They even gave the wrong national final exams in the high schools. Students won't graduate for another year! Another year for those children in the school yards....They'll end up like Sicelo." His anger ripples across his face as his torrent is spent. He clenches and unclenches his jaw.

"Read this," Mrs. Dube hands us a newspaper, The Echo *of Pietermaritzburg. Headline: YOUTH LEADER KILLED. I scan the article: eighteen-year-old Sicelo Dlomo...dead...murdered four days after police seized and questioned him about his appearance in the film, "Children of Apartheid."*

"It could be our Bonga next...," Mrs. Dube's breath seems short.

Mr. Dube, calmer, continues his wife's thought, "Though the facilities are better in Bonga's school here—a library, a sportsfield, toilets, better-qualified teachers, what good are these things if the teachers are afraid to come to school and the bathrooms are butcheries? We're sending our son to a rural school."

My mind snaps back to our rural school, Cebisa, at Mfanefile. Cebisa with overflowing classrooms. Cebisa with a shortage of teachers. Cebisa without water. Cebisa without electricity. Cebisa

without a playing field. Cebisa without a roof! Cebisa is better?
Yet better Bonga alive with a poor education than....

While South African education is upheld as the great liberalizer, it has actually been the great oppressor. Education has become synonymous with schooling, and schooling has effectively supported the apartheid structure. The state, through prescribed method and curriculum, defined truth and trained its population to believe and uphold this so-called truth. In many ways education as a public institution has become as much an opiate of the people as the institution of religion has ever been.

In a blatant (and very successful) attempt to make truth inaccessible to the people of South Africa, the Bantu Education Act and other laws separated children of different racial and ethnic groups. South African children not only have not lived together, they have not schooled together. Based on the philosophy of "own affairs" and "separate development," the white government created separate school systems, pre-primary through post-graduate, for each racial and ethnic group. By fostering intellectual underdevelopment and dependency in the black community, this segregated schooling perpetuated the unjust and oppressive apartheid philosophy and its practical implementation.[16]

Within the constraints of apartheid, many upheld that the solution to the discrepancy between schooling for white Africans and schooling for black Africans was to improve the schools for black Africans. But better schools for black Africans still meant separate state schools. With the state being white in composition, the "power-over" relationship continued.

Rather than being a tool in the search for truth, schooling for black Africans and white Africans has been a tool controlled by the white government and used to perpetuate the myths of apartheid. One example of this control is a 1989 ban in the white schools throughout the entire Transvaal province of all literature from Black Sash and several other anti-apartheid organizations. None of their publications were allowed on school grounds.

Under apartheid, education came to mean schooling for conformity and control. Not only the black community suffered. The white community suffered, too. In addition to being isolated from the majority of the country's population, the whites were separated amongst themselves by culture and language, Afrikaans from English. In all communities, there was little freedom for parents, teachers, or pupils to exercise any influence over their state schooling.[17]

The education acts of South Africa and the subsequent schooling systems have been, in effect, blocks to the Learning Spirit of individuals and communities. Key factors in the oppressive function of schooling in South Africa have been ideological, financial, spatial, staffing, and structural. According to the Education Affairs Act (which governed white schooling), the national Superintendent General's department had authority over every classroom in the Republic. It set the curriculum, selected the teachers and principals, and exercised disciplinary powers over all employees. Thus, the local school's political teachings and attitudes were under the direct control of the national department, and teachers could be disciplined for "misconduct," which included "encouraging disobedience or resistance to an act of Parliament, [and] public criticism of the administration of any State department."[18]

Apartheid in the schools mirrored the apartheid of the wider society. It socialized the children into a passive acceptance of apartheid as "the way it is."

Some enlightening statistics were published in 1988:[19]

1) Only three percent of black African teachers have a teacher training degree.

2) In 1988 student vacancies in white schools numbered 153,673 and were increasing. The vacancies by law could not be filled by black African students.

3) Even though the Department of Education and Training (the body overseeing black African schooling) admitted their need for fifty thousand additional trained teachers by the year 2000 and additional facilities to meet this training demand, fully equipped whites-only training colleges were being closed down.

(In March 1990, nine white government training schools closed in the Transvaal due to declining pupil enrollment, because the law did not allow "nonwhites" to attend white government schools.)

Economics, like schooling, is used to block and hide truth. The primacy of money, its value in and of itself, has been promoted effectively by primarily capitalist and "free" market economic principles. These principles often distort and sometimes explicitly deny actual circumstances. That money is a human invention and that the earth once existed without a price tag on it are well-kept secrets from the average person.

God's Anger Rages Throughout This Land

"One hundred and thirty-one rands."

Gogo Shandu and I sit dumbfounded by this proclamation. We arrived an hour ago to fetch five-year-old Sibusiso, who was admitted to the hospital two weeks ago with a high fever. The fever has left, though no diagnosis has been confirmed, and now Sibusiso is ready to go home. But one hundred and thirty-one rands! That's about sixty American dollars, a lot of money anywhere. For Gogo Shandu that translates into three or four months of food for herself and her two grandsons who live with her. The hefty staff nurse smiles, "Some people owe more than two hundred rands," she says, "and they have to stay until they pay. Then they owe six rands more each day. We don't know what they will do." Her face is dark against the white walls of the hospital room. Her voice, light and pleasant, holds a touch of frustration.

"The wards are empty: only six in the children's ward, only nine in the women's ward with forty-five beds. People are staying at home and dying because they are afraid of the hospital fees....What can they do?" She busies herself with the meal tray, distributing simple meals of cornmeal, gravy, and one or two cubes of beef. Sibusiso eats his meal heartily.

I end up in the superintendent's office. The superintendent is such a jolly looking Englishman, a bit of St. Nick in his rosy cheeks.

"The fee represents only one-fifteenth of the actual cost," the superintendent assures me. "The patients need to begin to help meet these costs, thus the increase in fees. They must learn this all doesn't just grow on trees."

"How ironic," I think to myself, "that many medicines do come from trees!"

"Some people cry 'poor' but really can afford the fees," he continues. "If there's a case of dire poverty, we arrange an account for payment."

How quickly we forget that cost is relative, not absolute. How quickly we forget that things cost only what those who control them determine their worth to be. How differently things would cost if the well-being of the consumer was paramount, rather than just the lining of the pockets of the producers.

God's anger rages through this land.

- *It costs too much to save children, but not too much to shoot them.*
- *It costs too much to shelter people, but not too much to bulldoze their homes.*
- *It costs too much to educate youth, but not too much to print myriads of government propaganda.*
- *It costs too much.*

Yes, the superintendent will see to arranging an account for the Shandus. Yes, we can take Sibusiso home today. "I don't really expect her to pay off the account, but 'they' must know how much things really cost," the superintendent ushers me out of his office.

I cringe at his use of the term "they," as if people-of-color are somehow innately different from people-without-color. This terminology appears so harmless, yet is truly destructive as it works to separate and polarize people.

What the superintendent does not realize, I think to myself, is that Gogo Shandu has a sense of integrity and will struggle for years to pay off this account, rand by rand, even if it means sacrificing such luxuries as new uniforms for school, washing soap powder, toothbrushes, and toothpaste, or another visit to the hospital for future medical needs. Until the account is officially closed, it will gnaw at her.

South Africa boasts of its subsidized health care for black Africans. The government waves the grand totals of these subsidies in front of the international and national press. But here in rural Zululand the realities sink in. What good are millions of rands of subsidy if people avoid the hospital because of the fees that remain? To someone like Gogo Shandu, last in line for her son's wages of four rands per day ($1.75), what real difference does the subsidy make? To her 131 rands might as well be 1,031 rands or 10,031 rands! It is too much.

Sibusiso and Gogo Shandu await my return to the ward. The clouds have removed the sunlight from the hospital walls, which now look dingy. Flies feast on the streaks of gravy on the lunch plates not yet collected.

Sibusiso does not look back to bid farewell to nurses or fellow patients. He scurries outside, glad to be going home, glad to be alive. I hope and pray that it will be a long time before he has to return.

———————

Economics reflect a society's priorities and values. The medical system in South Africa illustrates the practical consequences of the economy of apartheid. Those with the least political and economic power received the poorest facilities and care, while some of the best hospitals in the world were provided for whites.[20] The first heart transplant in the world was performed in a whites-only hospital in Cape Town. In 1983, there was one doctor providing the care for every 330 whites, while there was one doctor providing the care for every 12,000 black Africans.[21] Economic power is directly connected to political power, and the reciprocal is also true.

So what is truth?

Truth is relative. We must determine if what is upheld as true is genuine truth or a lie created to uphold a myth. We must examine its content: its source, its purposes, and its consequences. We must continuously re-examine our own suppositions, our framework, and the things we hold true, ever moving out of the shadows into the light of truth.

A life dedicated to the search for and proclamation of truth must be one of both surrender and discipline: surrender to the workings of the Learning Spirit, and a disciplined willing response to its urgings. It must adopt a willingness to change and the discipline not to disengage, not to live a life of deception.

This willingness is sensed as trust: trust of the urgings of the Learning Spirit; trust in the presence of God; trust of the process of change; trust that we can cope with the revealed realities; and trust that we can endure the pain we will necessarily face in the confrontation with truth about ourselves and our world. As Simone Weil writes, "The student of truth is not to set out on a search, but to be ready to receive naked truth."[22]

Notes

[1]T.S. Eliot, "Four Quartets," *Burnt Norton* (New York: Harcourt, Brace & Company, 1943), I.

[2]"Ribeiro Killings: Former Selous Scout Named," *Natal Mercury* (Durban, South Africa), July 1990, sec. 1, p. 2. The text of the article reads: "The commission is anxious to question Noel James Robey, who was cleared of involvement in the murders at a preliminary hearing in the Pretoria North Magistrate's Court in 1987. Until six months ago, the Rhodesian bush war veteran was a member of the SADF's Special Forces....[T]he *Sunday Times* learnt that the commission's investigation team confiscated certain documents....Former CCB member Willie van Deventer claimed in a newspaper report from London some months ago that he had information implicating the CCB in the Ribeiro killings."

[3]See Kairos Theologians, *The Kairos Document: Challenge to the Church: A Theological Comment on the Political Crisis in South Africa* (Braamfontein, South Africa: The Kairos Theologians, 1986), 3, for a discussion of State Theology.

[4]See Ross Snyder, *On Becoming Human: Discovering Yourself and Your Life World* (Nashville: Abingdon Press, 1967), 144.

[5]See K. Patricia Cross, *Adults as Learners: Increasing Participation and Facilitating Learning* (San Francisco: Jossey-Bass Publishers, 1982), 232. Cross describes this experience, "Most academics have had experiences where something 'clicked' and the learning changed suddenly from additive learning to transformed learning, in which the subject was seen from a new perspective. Most creative thought seems to be of this nature....It is not that the individual with the new idea has more content than anyone else but, rather, that he or she has put it together in new ways that transformed the idea."

[6]*Inclusive Language Hymns*, hymn 441, verse 1 (Amherst, Massachusetts: The First Congregational Church, 1984).

[7]*Ibid.*, verse 2.

[8]*Ibid.*, verse 3.

[9]For further descriptions of specific apartheid laws and their historical context, see Harold D. Nelson, ed., *South Africa: A Country Study*: Foreign Area Studies (U.S. Government: Secretary of the Army, 1981).

[10]See T.R.H. Davenport, *South Africa: A Modern History* (Toronto: University of Toronto Press, 1977), 298.

[11]Diakonia, *Education for Freedom: What Is the Churches' Role in the 1990's?* (Durban, South Africa: Diakonia, 1990), 7.

[12]Roger Omond, *The Apartheid Handbook: A Guide to South Africa's Everyday Racial Policies* (Middlesex, England: Penguin Books, Ltd., 1985), 73.

[13]Kairos Theologians, *The Kairos Document: Challenge to the Church: A Theological Comment on the Political Crisis in South Africa* (Braamfontein, South Africa: The Kairos Theologians, 1986), 6.

[14]Archdiocese of Durban, *Guardian of the Light*: *Tributes to Archbishop Denis Hurley OMI* (Durban, South Africa: Archdiocese of Durban, 1989), 66.

[15]*Ibid.*, 19.

[16]See Mokubung O. Nkomo, "The Contradictions of Bantu Education," *Harvard Educational Review* 51 (Feb. 1981),132.

[17]Ken Hartshorne, "Education—The Laboratory of South Africa's Future," *Sash: Special Education Focus* 31 (Mowbry, South Africa: Black Sash, Sept. 1988), 9.

[18]Roger Burrows, "Education Affairs Act: More Control," *Sash: Special Education Focus* 31 (Mowbry, South Africa: Black Sash, Sept. 1988), 27.

[19]See Betty Davenport and Mary-Louise Peires, eds., "Introduction," *Sash: Special Education Focus* 31 (Mowbry, South Africa: Black Sash, Sept. 1988), 4.

[20]"Factsheet 24" compiled and distributed by the Pietermaritzburg Agency for Christian Social Awareness (PACSA) provides helpful statistics about the fragmented health care system of South Africa.

[21]Roger Omond, *The Apartheid Handbook*, 71.

[22]Sr. Nancy M. Malone, O.S.U., "Paying Attention: Simone Weil on Education," *Commonweal* (9 April 1983), 197.

5

THE LEARNING SPIRIT HELIX: TRUST

The Cock Crowed Thrice

Our windows frame the hot stretches of Botswana. It has been a good week, a time to renew acquaintances and to build friendships, a time of clarification and vision. Now my family and I are heading home, back into the Republic of South Africa.

We near the border crossing post. Ahead of us on the South Africa side, two vans stand empty while the passengers, delegates from our church Assembly, are seemingly relaxing in the shade, waiting for approval from the guards to proceed. We nestle our car into the queue on the Botswana side, climb out, and proceed toward the passport control office. We pass through easily, and proceed to the South Africa side.

The South African clerk hands us the re-entry papers to complete and directs us to a writing counter like those found in post offices. We commence the laborious process. Not having committed our car license plate number to memory, I leave the room to check it. As I bend over the car, using the trunk as a writing desk, I

91

hear a quiet, "Hello." I turn, and a smile spreads across my face as I recognize the delegate from Port Elizabeth.

"The South African police searched our bags and came across the minutes of the Assembly," she whispers. "While thumbing through the papers, they found the resolution condemning the South African Defense Force. We didn't even think about that. Now we must wait while they take apart the vans and search thoroughly. I don't know what they think they'll find. We'll likely be held up for hours. You should hide your papers. Pretend you don't know us. Say you were on holiday in Gaborone." She abruptly turns and walks back to the group waiting in the shade.

I open the trunk and bury our church reports beneath diapers and the baby carriage. Then I return to the office to complete the forms. I think about the resolution.

The annual Assembly of the United Congregational Church of Southern Africa, which we had been attending, officially condemned the South African Defense Forces' (SADF) attack on Gaborone five months ago.

The invasion was reported to us by Henry Unrau, a Mennonite missionary serving as a radio broadcaster in Gaborone.[1]

...One o'clock in the morning, June 14, 1985...the SADF secretly cross into Botswana, drive to the small capital, Gaborone, and locate ten homes scattered across the city: ten homes targeted for destruction because, the South African government claims, these homes are occupied by trained African National Congress (ANC) terrorists.

The SADF soldiers call out into the darkness, ordering the occupants of the homes to come out. Some do, with their hands in the air, but they are gunned down by the soldiers. Others try to hide inside, but the soldiers throw bombs, killing some and wounding others. Then the soldiers enter the houses shooting at anyone still alive. Finally, as the SADF departs, demolition charges are set in each of the ten homes, and the buildings are leveled. In all, twelve people are killed, including a seventy-year-old man and a ten-year-old boy. The wounded number fourteen, including a pregnant woman.

The church Assembly adopted the resolution unanimously. We had condemned this act of war that South Africa, in its defense of apartheid, had struck against Botswana.

...We complete our re-entry forms declaring that we have been in Gaborone on business. We step outside.

Our twenty friends, still being held by the South African police, look at us, a brief flicker of recognition but no exchange of words.

As we wait, Amy, now fifteen months old, spots a woman in the group being held who had befriended her during the Assembly. Amy waddles over to her, and the woman automatically greets Amy by taking her into her arms and giving a big, "Hello." Those around us wait to see if the police will notice the obvious familiarity. But they are too busy searching the vans to see.

We collect Amy and drive the few yards to the search area. A police officer asks if we have any books or pamphlets. I reply by showing him my journal. He is not interested.

The search is over. The trunk is closed.

"Just pretend you don't know us."

We drive away, never looking back. And the cock crows for us. In our denial of our friends and our church, we feel like Peter, denying the truth. "She said again to those standing around, 'This fellow is one of them.' Again he denied it....Immediately the rooster crowed....Then Peter remembered the word Jesus had spoken to him....And he broke down and wept" (Mark 14:69b–70a,72).

Our fellow delegates are held for more than five hours. All of their church documents are confiscated.

Yes, we have been delivered from seemingly unnecessary hardship, since there was no need for us to stay, too. Perhaps we should consider ourselves "lucky" since we were not held at the border. And really, it is best not to get involved. The tiny voice of righteous justification consoles me.

But the Learning Spirit confronts me. Have we not denied truth merely for personal gain? Are Tod and I let through without a search because we are white? (The twenty delegates traveling by van are so-called coloreds.)

Amy, in her loving acknowledgement of her friend, witnesses to the truth of which we are afraid. In her naiveté she has the "courage to be," the willingness to trust in the moment.
Tod and I detect a heavy feeling of bitterness in ourselves. I sense these feelings are powerful indicators of our failure, our denial, our avoidance of creative participation in the moment, and thereby in genuine learning. We regret that we had not stayed in solidarity with the other delegates, trusting in God's presence with us.

———

Trust is the second strand of the helix of the Learning Spirit. As we consider its meaning and expression, we must always keep in mind its interrelatedness with the other two strands of the helix—truth and creative action—and willingness. As we encounter truth and move into trust, we become willing to take creative action.

Jesus of Nazareth succinctly describes this interrelatedness, "I tell you the truth, if you have faith [trust] as small as a mustard seed, you can say to this mountain, 'Move from here to there' and it will move. Nothing will be impossible for you" (Matthew 17: 20b–21).

Trust is a feeling, known in its certainty only to the individual in question. To all appearances I can be trusting, but internally fear can be in control. Alternately, I can appear fearful while internally sensing a foundation of trust.

Trust, and the surrender that is part thereof, can be experienced in a limited capacity. We can experiment by surrendering certain aspects of our lives or of the attitudes we hold. These limited surrenderings need not be fortified with great amounts of trust. In fact, such experimentation with trusting can result in confrontations with truth that boost our trust in a spiritual power. It is like opening a door a slight crack to see if any light shines through. When the light does shine through, we are encouraged to open the door wider. When we experience any amount of insight through even a partial engagement with the Learning Spirit, our trust in the possibilities of further engagement of the Learning Spirit increases.

The experience of trusting is an experience of movement, movement in a direction away from where we have been and toward something new. This experience of trusting, this new life of the spirit, frees us from our preoccupation with achievement, affluence, and appearance. Our security is no longer found in areas measured by social standards but in the realm of the spirit. We are then empowered for life of and in the spirit.

Distrust manifests itself in feelings of insecurity, low self-esteem, and worthlessness. When we feel insecure or fearful we may misplace our trust in illusory things. This in turn often leads to increased feelings of insecurity and fear. We might place our trust in the physical and material realm: in money, fame, academic achievement, social status, our physical strength or beauty, our nation's physical strength, alcohol, food, drugs, gambling. We might place our trust in the emotional realm: in love from our spouse or children, our sense of superiority over others, praise from our friends and colleagues.

It is not a new concept to suggest that trust in worldly things is illusory. We hear about the emptiness of the lives of those who have fame and fortune. It is plastered across the cover pages of scandal sheets and magazines. The prophets of the Hebrew Scriptures, like the prophets of our own time, warn the people against trusting in idols.

Yet, we continue looking for the ultimate fix, whether in our personal lives or in our corporate lives. We want the ultimate material protection against our enemies, real or imagined. We want the ultimate learning package to protect us against ignorance. We want the ultimate family situation to fulfill our every need.

When these ultimates let us down, as they often do, our attitudes and behaviors may become controlled by fear and self-preservation. We are likely to turn to substitutes to fill the void: e.g. alcohol, food, gambling, drugs, sex. Self-help groups are flourishing, not only in the United States but around the world, because they offer a response to this common let-down experience.

We may sense in ourselves an emptiness, a void, an insecurity, but we go blindly forward. We ignore the truth, hoping this time we will find the ultimate fix.

Contemporary western culture, with its emphasis on the separation between the physical, emotional, and spiritual realms, has convinced us that the answers for which we search must lie in either the physical or emotional realms. The spiritual realm has been categorized as untrustworthy, and is usually discounted as implausible. Yet when we place our trust in a spiritual power greater than ourselves, greater than any physical, material, emotional, or intellectual reality, we are catapulted into a new reality. We experience a new sense of ultimate security and trust as new relationships are established with ourselves, with others, and with God.

Here's Talking to You, God!

"I feel silly and don't really want to do this, and I don't even think you're real, but Phyllis tells me I must try. So, God, I'm talking to you."

I sit in my kitchen reaching out for the first time to a God I don't know. My spiritual guide, Phyllis, has urged me to set aside my pride and ask for help. Thus, the light of God's grace breaks through into my life.

As I turn my life and my will over to the care of God, as I understand God, the Spirit empowers me to clear away the wreckage of my past, to cut my chains, to be free, to chose life, to remove the dark lenses I have worn for so long.

I begin to trust in something new, in the presence of a spiritual power leading and directing me. I can neither see nor hear this power. But I boldly talk on, though I speak to no one. Such is the paradox of prayer. This spiritual power has become the Great Fact in my life. I write in my journal, "I have accepted a new faith, a new trust in a Higher Power, which I choose to call God."

Prayer is both a discipline and spontaneous conversation with the God in whom we trust. It is one gateway into the spiritual realm.

Prayer offers us the opportunity to slow down, to look around, to pause. When we pause, we hear the still whisper of the Spirit. In the quiet of prayer, we experience the presence of the Learning Spirit.

Prayer can facilitate our movement into trust. The resulting empowerment may provoke initially a sense of distrust and fear. Often the movement into profound trust is preceded by a period of distrust. We feel dissatisfied and agitated. Unfamiliar truth bursts forth into our reality at an unabsorbable rate. We find ourselves grappling and floundering. We may sense confusion or despair.

When our power of the Spirit is experienced and becomes familiar, we will trust in its presence and lean on its strength. A friendly and accepting spiritual power will provide the support and encouragement we need to move forward in faith and trust.[2]

Losers Win

Our God, our help in ages past, our hope for years to come.
Our shelter from the stormy blast, and our eternal home.[3]

"These guys are losers," I think to myself.
The smell of wood smoke from the fire is pungent and acrid. My eyes water as I sit down to escape the cloud that hangs at shoulder level in the mud and wattle hut. The curved wall is lined with wooden spoons and platters on display for the local handicraft buyer.

I fidget anxiously, awaiting the verdict. My eyes, now clear, are fastened on the carved platter being turned over in Baba (Mr.) Thala's hands for appraisal. But my mind is thinking over the string of failures I have seen the Mkwanazi family face.

First, there was Gogo (Grandmother) Mkwanazi, without a pension for ten years because her deformed right thumb would not yield a fingerprint. After a two-year struggle, we finally got her through the bureaucratic tangle. She died days after receiving her first pension check.

Then there is Jabu, the eldest son, who should be the hope of the family. Jabu was blinded by disease as a young man. Then there is Ngindi, an eight-year-old grandson, deaf and handicapped by cerebral palsy. The rehabilitation center refuses to enroll him because he is deaf; the school for the deaf refuses to enroll him because of his paralysis.

Then there is Alfred, in his early thirties, the younger son. Searching for permanent work over the years, he has traveled the circuit from Durban to Johannesburg. He squats now, crouched beside the fire. Furrows of futility crease his face—the same futility that seems displayed in the cracks of the dung floor where ants have pushed their way through and are making nests, only to be swept out each morning; the same futility that seems displayed in the dry ears of corn hanging from the ceiling like jagged-tooth grins. The same futility of the silence: no chickens cackling, no goats bleating, no bees droning in fruit trees...nothing.

"These guys are losers," I think to myself again. "Why did I ever bring Baba Thala here?"

Baba Thala stops fingering the wooden articles and, looking at Alfred, announces, "Mkwanazi, your work is beautiful. The spoons are the best I've seen. The traditional burned pattern is bold and sharp." His eyes hold respect for Alfred. "Let's talk. You are the factory, and I am the wholesaler. Now, let's see your tools."

I can hardly believe my ears. Mentally I had given up on this family. Alfred was a last hope, and I had hardened myself for yet another disappointment. These words of praise and promise have taken me by surprise. Alfred the loser has become Alfred the artist!

"Now faith is being sure of what we hope for and certain of what we do not see" (Hebrews 11:1). The futility of the previous moment dissolves.

Alfred displays his carving knife, its handle broken and taped, the blade looking as though it has been pressed in a waffle iron. His battered drill looks almost useless with its broken point.

"Use some of today's earnings to buy new tools," Baba Thala smiles. "I'm paying you twice the price you asked for. I try to pay fairly."

I walk home in a state of amazement. These "losers" are win-
ners. While my hope had died, they persevered in trust and faith
that the future is theirs, too. I realize that I must trust in something
greater than any process, greater than the people involved in the
process, even greater than the hoped-for outcome.

> *Our God our help in ages past, our hope for years to come,*
> *Be thou our guard while troubles last, and our eternal*
> *home.[4]*

Trust has both a physical component and an emotional component. Trust is usually accompanied by a sensation of physical serenity, a sense of incredible calm. Often it leads to a sense of empowerment, a surge of strength and courage. In the midst of turmoil and conflict, there is a "buoyancy, a welcoming and strengthening presence that meets us at our time of greatest fear and says,
'Take heart. It is I. Don't be afraid.'"[5] When we experience profound trust, we experience no trace of fear or trepidation. We let go
absolutely and experience surrender. This surrender is a felt experience. Yet it can be brought about by neither willpower nor reason.

I cannot convince myself to surrender to a higher spiritual power
and to engage the Learning Spirit. Only when I trust in the power,
only when I have experienced the reality of God, can I surrender to
it.

This moment or series of moments when we come into surrender, can be described as the moment of or the movement into conversion and transformation. We are transformed and move into a
new reality. We surrender ourselves to a call such as that expressed
by Paul in his letter to the Romans. Paul writes, "Do not conform
any longer to the pattern of this world, but be transformed by the
renewing of your mind" (Romans 12:2a).

This conversion is a personal reorientation, "a turning or re-
turning, a re-creation."[6] It is a radical change of direction away
from the unauthentic and fear toward authenticity and self-tran-
scendence. It involves the whole person: the intellectual, the emo-

tional, the physical, and the spiritual. When we undergo conversion, the power of our fears lessens and values are clarified and claimed. That which we know is shattered, and that which we have not known is made clear. Our world view is transformed and our relationships—with ourselves, with others, and with our higher power—change.

In no way is trust in the spiritual reality in opposition to the physical world. The spiritual is in relationship to the physical world and influences our being in it.

Sensing the presence of God and the establishment of trust, we sense the engagement of the Learning Spirit. The experience of buoyancy is the experience of trust, the experience of living in trust, the experience of living empowered by the Learning Spirit.

Face to Face

The stench of rotting meat is almost overpowering, and I feel suffocated in the dark hut. I inch nearer to the huddled form. The face, with skin pulled oddly across it by a massive burn scar, repels me. The frightened eyes seem to reflect the horror I feel.

I have been primed. Vusi, an epileptic, had a leg amputated when, a few years ago, in the throes of a seizure he rolled into a fire. Now he has again rolled into a fire, and his remaining leg has been burned. But I am not prepared for this—a young man about twenty-five years old, rotting alive! For days, perhaps for a week, Vusi's hope has been that the burns might heal. The hospital fee of six rands [about $2.40] per day has kept him home with this false hope. Now he will be lucky to keep the leg.

Accompanied only by my two-year-old daughter, I am unable to lift Vusi. His upper body is a mass of muscle. He makes his way on his strong arms and the stump of his amputated leg up the path to the car. Amy and I roll down all the windows, though the day is chilly, to minimize the stench.

At the hospital...

"He should have a permanent disability stamp in his pass-

book. Then he'd receive free treatment. I'll have to charge him full fees, because there's no stamp," the receptionist informs us.

After a discussion with the doctor-in-charge, it is agreed that the fees will be suspended. Vusi is admitted, and we are directed to make application for his disability stamp and pension at the district surgeon's office.

At the district surgeon's office...

"A letter from the hospital will be sufficient for his disability application, but this case must be reviewed in five years," the surgeon professionally proclaims.

We are shocked. "Doctor," replies Tod with as much calm as he can muster, "Vusi has no leg. Do you expect it to grow back in five years, or for that matter in ten or twenty?"

"Get the letter," barks the doctor.

Later that day, I return, letter in hand. The doctor disappears into his office enclave to complete the official form. His aide returns the form to me. As I peruse the form, surprise...the district surgeon has certified Vusi as permanently disabled, no review required. I feel victorious. We never see the doctor again.

At the magistrate's office...

"Vusi must come into our office to be fingerprinted," Mrs. Zwane, the social worker, flatly says. Her proclamation stuns me. I have explained that Vusi is in the hospital on intravenous feeding, possibly preparing for the amputation of his remaining leg. "He must come in himself," she firmly concludes.

Unwilling to accept this ludicrous request as the final decision, I become willing to speak personally with the magistrate, demanding that a solution be found. With apparent compassion and ease, the magistrate appoints the pension officer to visit Vusi in the hospital the very next day, and to take Vusi's fingerprints there. I sense another victory.

Three months later...Vusi is discharged from the hospital. They managed to save his leg, though it is badly damaged. There has been no notification from the magistrate's office regarding a pension or a disability stamp for his passbook. Vusi will wait, and wait, and wait.

Vusi's story is full of ripe pickings for the white South African looking for generalizations and myths by which to put down black Africans.

- *"They" cannot take care of themselves.*
- *"They" just let themselves go to the dogs.*
- *There is medicine for epileptics. He should have been taking it.*
- *"They" will do horrible things just to get sympathy and maybe some handouts. Things are not really as bad as "they" make them out to be.*
- *There are rules which must be followed. If one starts making exceptions, people will start taking advantage (thus the attitude of the hospital receptionist, the social worker, and the district surgeon).*

Whites, and others who scorn the conditions of the poor, do not live in comparable conditions. They avoid face-to-face encounters with the poor. They do not know the realities of having only open fires for cooking and heating. They do not know the reality of being unable to see a doctor because of lack of funds. They cannot comprehend being unable to store medicine because of lack of appropriate space. They are unfamiliar with the difficulties of refilling a medical prescription such as cost, transportation, and time.

I have encountered black African poverty face-to-face. Rather than conform to the prevailing attitudes held by whites about poor black Africans, I pray that through the power of the spirit I will remain open to truth. I pray that the spirit continue to empower me to act in trust.

> *Live in harmony with one another. Do not be proud, but be willing to associate with people of low position. Do not be conceited….Do not be overcome by evil; but overcome evil with good.*
>
> *Romans 12:16,21*

Those of us who come from "First World" nations, or from so-called developed communities within "Third World" nations, can be severed from our illusions and insular environment by face-to-face contact with people who live day-to-day in situations of genuine poverty. The engagement of our Learning Spirit depends, to a large degree, on our willingness to connect with people. Our liberation lies in our willingness to experience even a piece of life as lived by the oppressed of the world. As our awareness develops, as we encounter truth heretofore unknown to us, we either recoil in fear and horror, or we move into trust and welcome the Learning Spirit into our experiences and allow ourselves to be converted and transformed.

We are entrenched in our personal and social attitudes. We must leave our comfortable and secure material environment and openly confront the uncomfortable insecurity of the "Third World" environment. When we face the reality of that in which we have become entrenched, the ways in which we uphold oppressive attitudes and systems and selfish behavior, we can be jolted into a new reality, a new perspective, into the realm of the Learning Spirit. When we experience a face-to-face encounter with those we victimize by our attitudes or behavior, we can transfer our trust from "power over" to a higher power.

As we examine trust we must remember always to view it in relationship to the helix of the Learning Spirit. We must see it always in relationship to willingness, the willingness to examine truth, the willingness to experiment with degrees of trust, the willingness to open ourselves to surrender, the willingness to bracket our reality for the moment the Learning Spirit needs to engage itself. We must see trust always in relationship to truth, truth that bursts forth into our reality and jolts the uncommon into view, truth that introduces a new world outlook. And we must see trust always in relationship to creative action, the creative action that replaces our old attitudes and behaviors, the creative action we begin to demonstrate as our trust in a spiritual power, in God, grows.

Notes

[1]Henry Unrau, an unpublished report on the South Africa Defense Force invasion into Gaborone, Botswana, June 14, 1985.

[2]See William James, *The Varieties of Religious Experience* (New American Library: 1958).

[3]*Inclusive Language Hymns*, hymn 1, verse 1.

[4]*Ibid.*, verse 6.

[5]Eleanor Morrison, (Sermon preached at the ordination of Ana Gobledale into Christian ministry, 3 June 1982, Chicago, Illinois), 12.

[6]Paul Loffler, "Conversion in an Ecumenical Context," *The Ecumenical Review* 19 (July 1967), 258.

6

THE LEARNING SPIRIT HELIX:
CREATIVE ACTION

As the body without the spirit is dead,
also faith without actions is dead.
James 2:26(TEV)

And Who Is My Neighbor?

Early in the morning Philisiwe Khuzwayo knocks on the kitchen door asking, "Ana, have you any more yarn? I'm in the middle of crocheting a baby blanket." We find just enough, and she crochets while we share a pot of tea.

Mid-morning Baba Mthimkulu swings into our yard on his clunky old bicycle calling out, "Mfundisi! Mfundisi! Pastor! Pastor! Vusi Sibiya is very sick and needs to go to the hospital. Baba Sibiya is away and we have no transport. They won't take him on the bus. No one will help. Will you?"

The memory of my last trip to the hospital with one-legged Vusi is vivid. With his scars and unpleasant odor, the smell of despair and neglect, it is no wonder the community tends to isolate him.

"Let's go," I drive off with Baba Mthimkulu.

Before I return, Ma Dludla arrives, "Tod, the Zungu's baby died yesterday and they want the funeral tomorrow."

"How old was the baby?" Tod inquires.

105

"Four months. And they need a coffin," comes the reply.

As soon as I return from the hospital, having had Vusi admitted, Tod and Ma Dludla are off to town to purchase a coffin thirty-eight inches long.

Mid-afternoon, Zama, a teenage member of our church, stops by on her way home from school, her face swollen from a toothache. Do we have any aspirin? Yes. And we also manage to get her to the clinic to get the rotten tooth pulled.

In the late afternoon, Mpume Dube and I sit on a mat in our new round hut, exploiting the last rays of evening light to hem a skirt together. We laugh at the antics of the many children playing alongside us.

And now the chill of a late autumn evening descends upon our rugged hills. "Bye, Mom. Bye, Dad." With her stuffed blue backpack slung over her shoulders and her favorite doll, Mbali (Flower), tucked under her arm, my daughter, Amy, joins Thembi Nene. They race down the narrow, overgrown path leading to Thembi's home.

They disappear over the hill, above which I can just see the conical thatched roof of the Nenes' kitchen hut. It appears to steam as smoke escapes from the cooking fire burning inside.

Folks are scurrying home with bundles of wood atop their heads. We exchange greetings as they pass in front of the house. There is no moon tonight. Already it is very dark.

I can picture the Nenes' kitchen. Gogo (grandmother) Nene, her old cracked hands splitting reeds for the mats she will weave. Mjabuliseni, Thami, and Sabelo, the eldest of six brothers, tending the fire: hauling wood, cutting it, stoking the flames over which their mother cooks the evening porridge and around which others huddle, keeping warm. Amy will return tomorrow smelling like a cured ham; she has gone to spend the night with nine-year-old Thembi, her best friend.

"And who is my neighbor?" (Luke 10:29b).

Sometimes we get letters from the United States asking, "Don't you miss home?" White people in Melmoth sometimes ask, "What's it like to live out there all alone?" As if there are no people except ourselves at Mfanefile. As if we have no neighbors. As if we have no friends.

The underlying questions seem to be, "Can a place full of people so different from yourselves ever really be home? Isn't home where you're with people like yourself? Aren't you lonely being the only whites there?"

Mpume Dube, whose home is about eighty feet from our home, emerges from the darkness. "It's cold tonight," she remarks.

"Yes, very much," I reply.

"I can't connect the pipe on my gas bottle for my stove. I ran out of gas this morning. Now I'm trying to reconnect the pipe, but the top seems twisted. Can you help me?" she asks. Tod disappears into the darkness with her.

Do we miss home? We are home.

Are we lonely? Tonight our little girl is snuggled next to her best friend who is our neighbor.

Who is my neighbor? It is often the person right beside me whom I am blind to see because I am so busy looking for someone I will recognize, someone more like myself.

"Who is my neighbor?"

- *Thembi Nene is my neighbor.*
- *Gogo Nene is my neighbor.*
- *Mjabuliseni, Thami, and Sabelo are my neighbors.*
- *Philisiwe Khuzwayo is my neighbor.*
- *Baba Mthimkulu is my neighbor.*
- *Vusi Sibiya is my neighbor.*
- *Nokukhanya Dludla is my neighbor.*
- *The Zungus are my neighbors.*
- *Mpume Dube is my neighbor.*

These are my neighbors. I feel richly blessed. Through the love of strangers, a stranger in a strange land has been made welcome, made to feel at home.

―――――――――

Living at Mfanefile, I experienced an "unfolding," a freedom from much of the "First World" baggage I brought with me to South

Africa. Though I participated in the life, the death, the faith, and the doubt of my neighbors, initially I maintained a degree of distance. The myths of group identity and cultural chasms continued to strongly influence my thoughts and actions. Only after living in the Mfanefile community for almost five years did I open myself to the truth and allow myself to feel one with those around me. Only then did I trust the love that was being so freely offered to me. This blend of truth and trust enabled me to respond creatively, to respond in compassion, to respond not out of responsibility or obligation as the local pastor, but out of the knowledge and trust that I belonged.

Creative action is the third strand of the helix of the Learning Spirit. As with the other two strands, truth and trust, creative action must always be considered within the helix and in relationship to willingness. The experience of creative action always occurs within or as part of an experience of truth and trust. In the ever-spiraling helix of the Learning Spirit, creative action becomes a possibility when we sense a new freedom in our trusting relationship with a spiritual power and we become willing to act in faith.

When we become willing to get involved beyond merely responding to our own fears and limitations, we will begin to respond to the fears of others and the limitations placed on them by the structures of society and culture. We will feel compassion[1] and will participate in the experiences of suffering and oppression others have. We will uphold and move toward a vision of harmonious re-creation and renewal. Our actions will be in alignment with what we feel is for the good of our world.

The South African elections on April 27, 1994, came about because people transcended the laws and the ideology of apartheid. People were empowered by the Learning Spirit to reflect on and act in opposition to apartheid. To those who opposed apartheid, the truth of apartheid—the greed, fear, and selfishness upon which it was founded—had been revealed. To them a trust in a different vision, one of justice and unity, had been granted. Through them the creative action opposing the apartheid regime was orchestrated. In them we can see the Learning Spirit at work; it has been welcomed and incorporated into their lives.

Anglican Archbishop Desmond Tutu clarifies that which has liberated him and many others in the anti-apartheid movement to speak out and act in opposition to the destructive policies of apartheid. He writes:

> For many of us it is not our politics that constrains us to say and do what we do and say in opposition to apartheid and in working for a new South Africa. It is precisely our relationship with God, it is our worship, our meditation, our attendance at the Eucharist, it is these spiritual things which compel us to speak up for God, "Thus saith the Lord...", to be the voice of the voiceless. For many of us the spiritual is utterly central to all we are and do and say. It is precisely because we are turned first to God that God constrains us to turn toward our neighbor.[2]

When we move into trust and open ourselves to this call, creative action comes as a natural response. Driven by neither fear, nor guilt, nor obsession, our response will be creative and constructive.

If genuine conversion and transformation have occurred, if our trust is genuine, the change in who we are will extend beyond the intellectual realm, beyond merely a restructuring of our ideology. In our humility and service to others, we will manifest the creative love of God.

In the process of conversion we will move through a period of humble and tough questioning about ourselves and our relationships with others and with a higher power. We will face difficult decisions that may include:

- Am I willing to let go of my life as I now know it?
- Am I willing to see things differently?
- Am I willing to have the myths and lies I count on turned inside out?
- Am I willing to surrender myself to this unknown that confronts me?[3]

If we are to accept the call and move into creative action, there must be a truthful and trusting environment. The helix of the Learning Spirit must remain intact. Encountering the myths that temper and control our situations and having our minds and hearts illuminated by truth does not automatically lead us into the realm of the Learning Spirit and creative action. As Heraclitus wisely stated, "Much learning does not teach understanding."⁴ The willingness to take creative action occurs only when both truth and trust are present.

For many, this trust may never reach fruition, for they seek that which comforts and appeases and avoid that which confronts and challenges. Truth often both confronts and challenges. Consequently, it makes us uncomfortable. Only when we open ourselves absolutely to the Learning Spirit do we become willing to face any challenges to which we are called. Only then do we become willing to take risks for justice, freedom, and peace. We experience a fortitude of spirit and find ourselves humbled. We feel connected to the events and the people around us. We experience a sense of oneness, connectedness, commonality. The Learning Spirit engages us with the moment, with each of the components that make up that moment, and enables us to interact fully and creatively.

Sometimes the creative action one takes may appear trivial or insignificant on the grand scale of things, but for any of us the action may represent a major reorientation of our perspective and values.

God Painted the Sunset Pink

"I'd like my room to be pink."

My daughter's innocent request has sent me into a tailspin. I wonder from where my strong feelings arise. So what if my daughter wants a pink room! We asked what color she wants. She told us. What is the problem?

I remember my mother's comments about pink. Somehow the comments, the exact words of which I cannot remember, informed me that girls who wear pink dresses will not have a chance. They will not get a good job. They will *"just"* get married and mop *floors and change diapers forever.*

Looking at four-year-old Amy, I *"unlearn"* my childhood lesson. I am freed from my prejudice and stereotype. We paint her room pink.

In the days ahead I marvel at the magnificent evening skies at Mfanefile, for God has painted the sunsets pink.

Whether trivial or profound, creative action always aligns itself with movement toward freedom, reconciliation, and peace with justice. Though "trivial" creative acts may appear to show compassion only to the self, especially when compared to the impact of broader social creative action, they are not self-serving in the narrow sense. These acts represent a movement out of self, into a new relationship with oneself and one's environment and community. Seemingly trivial acts free us to function more fully in the world, free from historical, psychological, or other constraints. Sometimes seemingly trivial creative action can amaze us by being the seed or spark of a major social movement. An example of this is Rosa Park's simple yet profound decision to sit in the front of the bus, a decision that sparked the civil rights movement in the United States.

While I have not started a social movement, my experiences and new sense of trust have empowered me to experiment with my new freedom in areas of my life that previously had been clouded over by myths, fear, false-trust, the expectations of others, and my own greed. Some of these creative actions, acts of freedom, may seem trivial and only natural for a young adult. For me, however, in the movement of my life, in my conversion/transformation and the engagement of the Learning Spirit in my life, they are central and profound.

She Wore a Golden Gown

"Do you think it's OK if I wear the dress Phillipine sewed for me?"

"Sure. It looks great."

I feel uncomfortable wearing this dress that glitters with metallic thread. I wonder if it is too flashy for me, especially with the shiny gold belt. I think to myself, "My mother never would have worn anything like this."

Then in a bright moment of illumination, I open myself, mind and spirit. I set aside my preconceived notions about glittery apparel.

With clarity of vision, I realize that I can wear anything I want! I have received a gift from a friend, and I like it. I like it! It does not matter what hangs in my mother's wardrobe, or in anyone else's. This is my wardrobe. This is my day!

A new understanding of truth invades my reality. My trust is in the loving power that is opening my eyes. Now a new willingness enables me to begin to unravel the oppressive tendrils of my relationship with my mother. I sense a new courage and a new trust that together insist I can both examine and identify these tendrils. I begin to pull myself free from them.

Having started the process, I take further creative action. I move in freedom and joy.

After eight years of marriage, I take off my grandmother's wedding ring which my mother had given to me to wear as my own. My husband and I purchase matching rings for ourselves.

After doing needlework apologetically for years, I admit I enjoy it. I reject (unlearn) the notion that women who work needle and thread are somehow "less than." I enter my work in a local craft fair and smile when I view it on display.

I feel free, and it is a good feeling.

The everyday affairs of our homes, our families, our communities, and our block clubs can hold a greater degree of significance for our lives as genuine learning experiences than traditional "educational" events.[5] Often our formal "education" is removed and irrelevant to our immediate concerns. Our new perceptions of these everyday affairs can lead to our willingness to take creative action.

Abraham Maslow, an authority on learning and education, relates a fascinating account of a moment of personal insight. He is invaded by a new perspective and takes creative action.

If I were to list the most important learning experiences in my life, there come to mind getting married, discovering my life work, having children, getting psychoanalyzed, the death of my best friend, confronting death myself, and the like. I think I would say that these were more important learning experiences for me than my Ph.D. or any 15 or 150 credits or courses that I've ever had. I certainly learned more about myself from such experiences. I learned, if I may put it so, to throw aside many of my "learnings," that is, to push aside the habits and traditions and reinforced associations which had been imposed upon me. Sometimes this was at a very trivial, and yet meaningful, level. I particularly remember when I learned that I really hated lettuce. My father was a "nature boy," and I had lettuce two meals a day for the whole of my early life. But one day in analysis, after I had learned that I carried my father inside me, it dawned on me that it was my father, through my larynx, who was ordering salad with every meal. I can remember sitting there, realizing that I hated lettuce and then saying, "My God, take the damn stuff away!" I was emancipated, becoming in this small way me, rather than my father.[6]

The homely trivial events in our lives are ripe with experiences through which the Learning Spirit can reach out to us. We must be open to its arrival and be willing to welcome it in. When we allow ourselves to live in the present, to listen to the voice of the spirit and to trust it, we can be freed from the constraints of expectations, social norms, and the mother-knows-best syndrome. We can open ourselves to the Learning Spirit and become willing to take creative action.

As my trust in a spiritual power has developed, I have become empowered and encouraged to experiment more and more in the area of academia.

My Mind Is My Own

"Participatory Education is not something just to learn about. It's a way of thinking, a way of being together as instructor and students. We'll be using the participatory model in this course."

I listen to the instructor tell us what we are going to do, and how we are going to participate as equals.

Then he surprises me, "I require a final paper from each of you. I must have some grounds upon which to determine your grades."

"Wait a minute." Hot redness shoots up the back of my neck. I press on, "You're contradicting yourself. Either we're working on the participatory model or we're not. If we are, YOU can't decide unilaterally any of the rules."

I realize I am risking everything—failure, wasted money, disapproval of the professor. But I persist, "You relinquish your power, and we're your equals. We all decide if there's going to be a final paper. We all do the grading, too."

The course and my learning, I realize, are primarily my *concern and* my *responsibility, not his. It will be* my *grade, not his. I pay my tuition not to buy a grade, but to put myself into a situation with others in which I might share my ideas and be introduced to new ideas. And, I realize, there are other places where I need not pay for such a situation!*

I am free to take creative action. I can challenge the instructor, disagree with him, refuse to be manipulated into a pseudo-participatory model. I can even get up and leave if I feel dissatisfied. I own the moment, as I pray, "God, give me courage and wisdom."

———

When we open ourselves to the Learning Spirit, we become clear about our values, courageous in upholding them, and bold in promoting them. The myths that have controlled us burst apart or wither into nothingness. The powers-that-be no longer determine our thoughts and behavior. We are free. Free to denounce old ways of thinking and behaving. Free to be converted and transformed into something new, someone new. Free to live fully in the Now.

I Don't Need Another "A"

"I'm dropping out."

"Are you sure you want to?"

"Yes. I'm sure."

I realize I do not want to be a student anymore. It has been the way I have found self-worth in the past, but I realize I do not need it anymore. I do not need another "A" or another degree.

I have learned that a prime motivating factor behind my desire to achieve academically has been my desire to please my father. He has been my idol, my higher power. My desire for his approval and affirmation has motivated me over the years to achieve and excel. Now I have a new higher power that is calling me to let go of the familiar ladders of success. This spiritual power is calling me to something new, something unknown.

I act in the freedom this newly revealed truth offers. Transferring my trust away from my father's approval to a spiritual power, I leave the degree program in which I am enrolled and head to Africa as a missionary.

As long as we remain willing to continue in the creative life, led and prompted by the Learning Spirit, our lives will never be the same. We will be transported into a new reality, a new way of living. This altered manner of living does not come easily. To walk the road of truth, trust, and creative action demands great effort and determination. But the willingness and courage to persist is available through the simple acts of opening ourselves and surrendering to the Learning Spirit.

When we encounter truth and stand in trust, our actions will be creative and compassionate. We find ourselves buoyed by a courage and determination before unknown to us. We find ourselves concerned with those around us, no longer afraid to risk the comforts and securities we had thought so essential to our own happiness. We are lifted up "as on the wings of eagles."

There is no human situation that does not present possibilities for action higher than the conventional and traditional customs and habits of people. When one encounters truth and moves into the experience of trust, one will sense the call to creative action. This call demands a response. Empowered by the Learning Spirit, we will begin to be instruments for the expression of creative action, instruments of God's Spirit. We will accept the radical and disturbing call of the spirit to act for freedom, justice, and peace in each and every situation we find ourselves.

Notes

[1]See Donald P. McNeil, Douglas A. Morrison, and Henri J.M. Nouwen, *Compassion: A Reflection on the Christian Life* (Garden City, New York: Image Books, Doubleday & Co., Inc., 1983), 124.

[2]Bishop Desmond Tutu, "Foreword," in *Cry Justice: Prayers, Meditations and Readings from South Africa*, ed. John De Gruchy (London: Collins Liturgical Publications, 1986), 12-13.

[3]See Richard Shaull, "Liberating Ourselves: Recovering the Gospel for North America," *The Other Side* 25 (Sept/Oct 1989), 46.

[4]Cited in *For Today*, Overeaters Anonymous, 263.

[5]Eduard C. Lindeman calls experience and the education that arises from it "a homely matter." See Eduard C. Lindeman, *The Meaning of Adult Education*, 87.

[6]Abraham H. Maslow, "Some Educational Implications of Human Psychologies, *Harvard Educational Review* 38, (Fall 1968), 691.

7

In Conclusion:
Living in the Spirit

Education is not a preparation for life;
education is life itself.[1]

And This Shall Be a Sign

The *persistent knock on the door rouses me. I rise and wrap my robe around me. When I open the door, two church members, Khanisiwe Mhlongo and Philisiwe Nene, emerge from the darkness and cold of the bleak midwinter morning.*

"A baby is about to be born!" they excitedly herald the news. As I dress, Amy and Mandla awaken. We delight in this excitement on the dawn of Amy's sixth birthday.

We pile into our car, Amy and Mandla, too. With one of the few cars in our community, we are often called upon to serve as an ambulance service to the hospital five miles away.

Stopping beside the home, I wait with my children while Philisiwe and Khanisiwe go to fetch the mother-to-be whom I do not know. Amy taps my shoulder. "She's calling you," she whispers and points toward the home.

Now I hear Philisiwe calling urgently, "The baby's coming out." I scurry up the slope, through the wire fence and into the candlelit hut. I am not sure what help I will be, but, trusting in God, I am willing to do what I can.

117

The baby's head is crowning. Luckily for me and the woman in labor, we are not alone. Gogo (grandmother) Mhlongo takes charge. She calls for towels and water. As I hand her a towel, the baby's head emerges, quickly followed by two slippery shoulders. The baby slides out. A little grey heap. Is it alive? There seems to be a lot of blood.

The candle flickers in a cold breeze that blows in around the single window. The stars are fading with the dawn.

I cringe upon seeing the piece of broken bottle Gogo Mhlongo will use to cut the cord. A prayer is murmured, placing our trust in God, as Gogo Mhlongo ties strings to the cord and saws until it is severed.

The stillness seems to go on and on....Then, a cry...life!

Smiles emerge all around. I am exhilarated to have witnessed such a miracle of creation, and am grateful that this wee one has managed, so far, to overcome all the obstacles facing a baby born black and poor in South Africa. I wrap the baby, a boy, in a towel. We urge the mother on. (I have learned that her name is Ncane which means "little one.") Gogo Mhlongo massages Ncane's stomach. The afterbirth is released and Ncane lies quietly.

Mandla and Amy watch from the shadows in the corner. Amy beams with pride to be sharing her birthday with this newborn.

I recall Amy's birth, such a contrast to this one. I remember the clean hospital. I remember the lights of the operating room, the masked faces of the medical team, the shiny metal equipment.

The new life is bundled in a towel, swaddling cloths, and placed on his mother's breast. Mother and child rest.

Outside in the rosy morning light we share a prayer of thanksgiving. A voice penetrates my being, "And this will be a sign for you,...You will find a babe wrapped in swaddling clothes lying in a manger. Emmanuel! God is with us!"

In the stillness I think of that birth so long ago we celebrate so sterilely each Christmas. We forget that the conditions of Jesus's birth were more like this—in a poorly lit, crowded room with a dung floor—than like our high-tech hospital or home birthings. I wonder what fires heated water for Jesus's birth, what towels were there to clean mother and child? What tool was used to sever his umbilical cord?

I return to the side of mother and child, both sleeping now. Indeed, God is with us. God has come to live among us as a human being, arriving as a helpless baby. Each day in our world, in God's creation, babies are born, each one bringing the hope of the Messiah come again, each one adding to God's promises that all things will be created new.

"And this will be a sign for you...."

The act of opening ourselves to the Learning Spirit and the engagement of the Learning Spirit are not in preparation for life; they are the experience of becoming fully alive. When we pass from one situation to another, open to the urgings of the Learning Spirit, our environment will expand. When we obstruct the Spirit's engagement, our environment will contract. This choice, to open ourselves or close ourselves, continues throughout our lifetime.

Genuine education is the process of opening and changing. Genuine learning and education are things of the spirit. Engagement of the Learning Spirit opens us to truth, grounds us in trust, and thereby shapes and reshapes our world. Genuine education occurs, and we come to know about ourselves and our world. We then act creatively in response to this knowledge.

Genuine education happens not only in structured educational settings but in the quiet of a moment. It is the insight or revelation we have that leads us to change, those moments in life when things "click." This learning may be experienced as a homely and seemingly trivial insight, or as a profound and challenging confrontation with our values, lifestyle, and beliefs. It may occur in the midst of a familiar and mundane activity such as eating lettuce or choosing the color to paint a room. Or this life-altering learning may occur during a dramatic face-to-face encounter with another person, with birth or with death.

The following poem eloquently encapsulates the essence of genuine education, the essence of life when the Learning Spirit is engaged.

Education Is Change[2]

Education is change—
sometimes subtle, sometimes cataclysmic—
in the consciousness of a person...
and thus in the structures Humanity has evolved
to define and extend itself.
Education doesn't happen through bureaucratic teaching
Through perfunctory learning.
Education is never impersonal or artless or cold.
Education has to do with Humanity becoming
Aware
To learn
To take effective action
To improve the condition of human beings in the world
And one's self.
But since
The world is large. History is long.
And the sum total of human
Knowledge is infinite
Disciplined understanding is essential
To change
The world
And ourselves.
We begin
With respect
For ourselves
For each other
And
For all that can be learned.

My experience of apartheid in South Africa jolted my reality. Truth about the world and how I must relate to it broke forth and changed my life forever. Now, living in the United States, I continue to be confronted by the truth about myself and my society. Reinserted into a familiar and comfortable environment, I find myself less open to the engagement of the Learning Spirit. Here in the United States, our racism appears more subtle; our poverty seems more remote; our greed seems more intensely institutionalized in our economy. I stand on the other side of the lens now, on the side of the oppressor, the side through which all the problems seem smaller. I am slower to doubt the lies propogated by the media. I am slower to recognize myths. I am more trusting of spokespersons of the status quo. But I trust in the spirit of truth and freedom, and pray to open myself to the learning it has in store for me.

Each of us can open ourselves up to the truth of our own context. We can be empowered by our trusting relationship with God to face the truth that confronts us. The Learning Spirit will nurture us, teach us, and guide us. We will genuinely learn the lessons that challenge us. We will be transformed.

A Guide by Which to Live and Learn in the Spirit

- Attend to my own issues, trying always to be open to the Learning Spirit, trying always to be willing to risk myself and my belief systems for something new.
- Trust in a spiritual power, in a guiding vision, and in wisdom.
- Share with others, not as the specialist or holder-of-knowledge, but as a kindred spirit and traveler on the journey of self-understanding.
- Recognize my own ignorance, racism, classism, sexism, nationalism, and elitism and be willing to acknowledge, to myself and to others, each aspect of my character.
- Strive to hear the voices of the oppressed, or to participate as one of those voices, and to undertake responsible action to dismantle the oppressive situation of the world in which we live.
- Find and carry out creative responses to the urgings of the Learning Spirit.
- Work for reconciliation, freedom, and peace with justice on both the personal level and the social level.
- Share my personal journey—my joys and tribulations—with others.

- Participate in a community of reflective and active persons.
- Listen.

Notes

[1]John Dewey, *Experience and Education* (New York: Collier Books, 1963), 44.

[2]Printed in a Goddard College brochure in the mid-1970s. Author unknown.

BIBLIOGRAPHY

This bibliography contains listings under the following headings: Education; Psychology and Philosophy; Theology and Spirituality; South Africa; and Other.

Education

Argyris, Chris. *Reasoning, Learning, and Action: Individual and Organizational.* San Francisco: Jossey-Bass, 1982.

Bergevin, Paul. *A Philosophy for Adult Education.* New York: Seabury Press, 1967.

Botkin, James W., Mahdi Elmandjra, and Mircea Malitza. *No Limits to Learning: Bridging the Human Gap: A Report to the Club of Rome.* Elmsford, New York: Pergamon Press, 1979.

Bruner, Jerome S. "The Act of Discovery." *Harvard Educational Review* 31, No. 1 (1961): 21-32.

_____. *The Relevance of Education.* New York: W.W. Norton & Company, 1971.

Burrows, Roger. "Education Affairs Act: More Control." *Sash:Special Education Focus* 32 (Sept 1988): 26-27.

Cross, K. Patricia. *Adults as Learners: Increasing Participation and Facilitating Learning.* Jossey-Bass Series in Higher Education. San Francisco: Jossey-Bass, 1982.

Darkenwald, Gordon G. and Sharan B. Merriam. *Adult Education: Foundations of Practice.* New York: Harper & Row, 1982.

Dewey, John. *Experience and Education.* New York: Collier Books, 1963. (Originally published by Kappa Delta Pi, 1938).

Diakonia. *Education for Freedom: What Is the Churches' Role in the 1990's?* Durban, South Africa: Diakonia, 1990.

Friere, Paulo. *Pedagogy of the Oppressed.* New York: Herder and Herder, 1970.

_____. "The People Speak Their Word: Learning to Read and Write in Sao Fome and Principe." *Harvard Educational Review* 51 (February 1981): 27-30.

Grabowski, Stanley M., ed. *Paulo Friere: A Revolutionary Dilemma for the Adult Educator.* Eric Clearinghouse Occasional Paper No. 32. Syracuse: Syracuse University, 1972.

Graves, Bingham. "What Is Liberating Education? A Conversation with Myles Horton." *Radical Teacher* (May 19, 1979): 3-5.

Groome, Thomas H. "Conversion, Nurture and Educators." *Religious Education* 76 (Sept-Oct. 1983): 482-96.

Gross, Ronald. *The Lifelong Learner.* New York: Simon & Schuster, 1977.

Guba, Egon G. *Toward a Methodology of Naturalistic Inquiry in Educational Evaluation.* Los Angeles: University of California Center for the Study of Evaluation, 1978.

Hartshorne, Ken. "Education—The Laboratory of South Africa's Future." *Sash: Special Education Focus* 31 (Sept 1988): 24.

Hawkins, Richard. "'Open' Schools Open Minds." *Sash: Special Education Focus* 31 (Sept 1988): 24.

Heaney, Thomas W. "Liberatory Adult Education in Traditional Schools or Can a Rabbit Catch a Fox?" *Proceedings of the 22nd Annual Adult Education Research Conference*, DeKalb, Illinois (April 1981): 103-8.

_____. "Politics of Explanation: The Ongoing Human Quest for Power." Paper presented at the Midwest Adult Education Research Conference, Northern Illinois University, October 1982.

Hiemstra, Roger. *Lifelong Learning.* Lincoln, Nebraska: Professional Educators Publications, Inc., 1976.

Houle, Cyril O. *The Inquiring Mind: A Study of the Adult Who Continues to Learn.* Madison: University of Wisconsin Press, 1963.

Illich, Ivan. *The Breakdown of Schools.* CIDOC CUADERNO, No. 1016. Cuernavaca, Mexico: Centro Intercultural de Documentation, 1971.

_____. *Deschooling Society.* New York: Harper and Row, 1971.

Kidd, J.R. *How Adults Learn.* New York: Association Press, 1973.

Knowles, Malcolm S. "Innovations in Teaching Styles and Approaches Based upon Adult Learning." *Education for Social Work* (Spring 1972): 32-39.

_____. *The Modern Practice of Adult Education.* New York: Association Press, 1970.

Knox, Alan B. *Adult Development and Learning.* San Francisco:Jossey-Bass, 1977.

Lindeman, Eduard C. *The Meaning of Adult Education.* New York: New Republic, 1926.

Malone, Sr. Nancy M., O.S.U. "Paying Attention: Simone Weil on Education." *Commonweal* (April 8, 1983): 196-97.

Maslow, Abraham H. "Some Educational Implications of Human Psychologies." *Harvard Educational Review* 38 (Fall 1968): 685-696.

Merriam, Sharan. "Philosophical Perspectives on Adult Education: A Critical Review of the Literature." *Adult Education* 27, No. 4 (1977): 195-208.

Mezirow, Jack. "A Critical Theory in Adult Education." *Adult Education* 32, no. 1 (1981): 3-24.

Nkomo, Mokubung O. "The Contradictions of Bantu Education." *Harvard Educational Review* 51 (Feb. 1981): 126-38.

Ohliger, John. *Bibliography for Adult Education.* Madison: Basic Choices, 1981.

_____. "Education and Society: Sparkling Adult Education." *Adult and Continuing Education Today* (Manhattan, Kansas) 18 (Nov. 21, 1988): 1.

_____. "What Is Radical Adult Education?" *Adult and Continuing Education Today* (Manhattan, Kansas) 20 (February 12, 1990).

Palmer, Parker. *To Know as We Are Known: A Spirituality of Education.* San Francisco: Harper & Row, 1983.

Patersen, R.W.K. *Values, Education and the Adult.* International Library of Philosophy of Education, edited by R.S. Peters. London: Routledge & Kegan Paul, 1979.

Ramos, Graciela and Victor Quintana. "Mexico: An Experiment on the Study of History." *Education Newsletter of the Office of Education.* (Geneva: World Council of Churches) No. 3 (1984): 5-7.

Rockhill, Katherine. "Researching Participation in Adult Education: The Potential of the Qualitative Perspective." *Adult Education* 33 (Fall 1982): 3-19.

Rogers, Carl R. *Freedom to Learn.* Columbus, Ohio: Charles E. Merrill, 1969.

Spear, George E. and Donald W. Mocker. "The Organizing Circumstance: Environmental Determinants in Self-directed Learning." Paper presented at the Midwest Adult Education Research Conference, DeKalb, Illinois, 1982.

Stanage, Sherman M. *Adult Education and Phenomenological Research: New Directions for Theory, Practice, and Research.* Malabar, Florida: Robert E. Krieger Publishing Co., 1987.

_____. "Meaning and Value: Human Action and Matrices of Relevance in Philosophies of Education." *Educational Theory* 26 (Winter 1976): 53-71.

Thorndike, E.L., et al. *Adult Learning.* New York: Macmillan, 1928.

Tough, Allen M. *Intentional Changes: A Fresh Approach to Helping People Change.* Chicago: Follett Press, 1982.

_____. *The Adult's Learning Projects: A Fresh Approach to Theoryand Practice in Adult Education.* Toronto: Ontario Institute for Studies in Education, 1971.

_____. *Why Adults Learn: A Study of the Major Reasons forBeginning and Continuing a Learning Project.* Monographs in Adult Education. Toronto: Ontario Institute for Studies in Education, 1968.

van den Heever, Randall, ed. *Alternative Education: Vision of a Democratic Alternative.* Cape Town, South Africa: Union of Teachers Associations of South Africa, 1987.

Psychology and Philosophy

Alcoholics Anonymous, Inc. *Alcoholics Anonymous.* New York: Alcoholics Anonymous World Services, 1938.

Arendt, Hannah. *Willing: The Life of the Mind II.* New York: Harcourt Brace Jovanovich, 1978.

Dewey, John. *Philosophy, Psychology and Social Practice.* New York: G.P. Putnam's Sons, 1963.

Erikson, Erik H. *Childhood and Society.* 2d ed. New York: W. W. Norton, 1963.

_____. *Identity: Youth and Crisis.* New York: W.W. Norton, 1968.

Findley, John Niemeyer. *Kant and the Transcendental Object: A Hermeneutic Study.* Oxford: Oxford University Press, 1981.

Fingarette, Herbert. *The Self in Transformation: Psychoanalysis, Philosophy, and the Life of the Spirit.* New York: Basic Books, 1963.

James, William. *The Meaning of Truth.* Cambridge: Harvard University Press, 1975.

_____. *The Varieties of Religious Experience: A Study in Human Nature.* New American Library, 1958. Originally published by Green and Company, New York, 1902.

_____.*The Will to Believe, and Other Essays in Popular Philosophy.* New York: Longmans, Green & Co., 1897.

Maslow, Abraham H. *Motivation and Personality.* New York: Harper and Row, 1954.

_____. *Toward a Psychology of Being.* 2d ed. An Insight Book, edited by David C. McClelland. New York: D. Van Nostrand Company, 1968.

Peck, M. Scott. *The Road Less Traveled: A New Psychology of Love, Traditional Values and Spiritual Growth.* New York: Simon and Schuster, 1978.

Pfänder, Alexander. *Phenomenology of Willing and Motivation.* Northwestern University Studies in Phenomenology and Existential Philosophy, ed. John Wild, trans. Herbert Spiegelberg. Evanston, Illinois: Northwestern University Press, 1967.

Ricouer, Paul. "Philosophy of Will and Action." In *Phenomenology of Will and Action*, edited by Erwin W. Straus and Richard M. Griffith. Pittsburgh: Duquesne University Press, 1967.

Rogers, Carl R. *On Becoming a Person.* Boston: Houghton Mifflin, 1961.

Spiegelburg, Herbert. "Phenomenology." *Encyclopedia Britannica.* Chicago: Encyclopedia Britannica, Inc., 1965.

_____. *The Phenomenological Movement: An Historical Introduction.* Hague: Nijhoff, 1960.

Wolff, Kurt H. *Surrender and Catch: Experience and Inquiry Today.* Boston Studies in the Philosophy of Science 51. Boston: R. Reidel, 1976.

_____. "Surrender and Catch." *Journal for the Scientific Study of Religion* 2 (1962): 36-50.

Zaner, Richard M. *The Disciplining of Reason's Cunning: Kurt Wolff's "Surrender and Catch."* Neuman Studies 4. Nashville:Vanderbilt University Press, 1981.

_____. *The Way of Phenomenology: Criticism as a Philosophical Discipline.* New York: Pegasus, 1970.

Theology and Spirituality

Boers, Arthur. "Faces of Faith: An Interview with Henry Nouwen." *The Other Side* 25 (Sept/Oct 1989): 14-19.

Brauer, Jerald C. "Conversion: From Puritanism to Revivalism." *Journal of Religion* 58 (July 1978): 227-43.

Brown, Robert McAfee. *Spirituality and Liberation: Overcoming the Great Fallacy.* Philadelphia: Westminster/John Knox Press, 1988.

Comblin, Jose. *The Holy Spirit and Liberation.* Translated by Paul Burns. Maryknoll, New York: Orbis Books, 1989.

Dear, John, S.J. "The Road to Transformation: A Conversation with Brian Willson." *Fellowship* (March 1990): 4-8.

Dewey, John. *A Common Faith.* New Haven: Yale University Press, 1934.

Hanh, Thich Nhat. "Enjoying Peace," *Fellowship* (March 1990): 8-9.

Inclusive Language Hymnal. Amherst, Massachusetts: The First Congregational Church, 1984.

Kairos Theologians. *The Kairos Document: Challenge to the Church: A Theological Comment on the Political Crisis in South Africa.* Braamfontein, South Africa: The Kairos Theologians, 1986.

Leech, Kenneth. *Experiencing God: Theology as Spirituality.* San Francisco: Harper & Row, 1985.

Loffler, Paul. "Conversion in an Ecumenical Context." *The Ecumenical Review* 19 (July 1967): 249-260.

McCrae, Ian, ed. *Global Sermon Notes*, No. 90-03. Indianapolis: Divisions of Homeland Ministries and Overseas Ministries of the Christian Church (Disciples of Christ), March 1990.

McIntosh, L.D. "John Wesley: Conversion as Continuum." *Midstream* 8, No. 3 (1966): 50-65.

McNeill, Donald P., Douglas A. Morrison, and Henri J. M. Nouwen. *Compassion: A Reflection on the Christian Life.* Garden City, New York: Image Books, Doubleday & Co., 1983.

Macquarrie, John. *Paths in Spirituality.* Student Christian Movement Press, 1972.

Martyn, Dorothy Watkins. "Compulsion and Liberation: A Theological View." *Union Seminary Quarterly Review* 36 (Winter/Spring 1981): 119-29.

Merton, Thomas. *New Seeds of Contemplation.* New York: New Directions, 1962.

Miller, Richard K. "A Call for a New Reformation." *The Disciple* (January 1990): 28-29.

Morrison, Eleanor. Untitled sermon preached at the ordination of Ana Gobledale into Christian ministry, Chicago, Illinois, June 3, 1982.

Niebuhr, Reinhold. *Faith and Politics: A Commentary on Religious, Social and Political Thought in a Technological Age.* New York: George Braziller, 1968.

Palmer, Parker J. *The Company of Strangers: Christians and the Renewal of America's Public Life.* New York: Crossroads, 1983.

Pilgrim Hymnal. Boston: The Pilgrim Press, 1958.

Rambo, Lewis R., "Current Research on Religious Conversion: A Bibliography," *Religious Studies Review* 8 (April 1982): 146-59.

Reuther, Rosemary Radford. "Theology of Liberation in Global Perspective." *Democratic Left* (July-Aug 1989): 11-12.

Shaull, Richard. "Liberating Ourselves: Recovering the Gospel for North America." *The Other Side* 25 (Sept/Oct 1989): 42-46.

Smith, John E. "The Concept of Conversion." *Midstream* 8, no.3 (1966).

Snyder, Ross. *On Becoming Human: Discovering Yourself and Your Life World.* Nashville, Tennessee: Abingdon Press, 1967.

_____. "Toward a Core Vocabulary." *The Chicago Theological Seminary Register* 80 (Spring 1989): 1.

Steere, Douglas V. *Gleanings: Selected Writings.* Nashville: The Upper Room, 1986.

Stuber, Stanley I., ed. *The Christian Reader: Inspirational and Devotional Classics.* New York: Association Press, 1952.

Tillich, Paul. *The Courage to Be.* New Haven: Yale University Press, 1952.

_____. *The Eternal Now.* New York: Charles Scribner's Sons, 1963.

Weaver, William N. "A Plea for Theological Humility." *Disciples Divinity House Bulletin* (Chicago) 59 (Fall 1989): 1, 3, 5-6.

Weil, Simone. "Reflections on the Right Use of School Studies with a View to the Love of God." In *The Simone Weil Reader* edited by George A. Panichas. New York: David McKay Company, 1977.

South Africa

Archdiocese of Durban. *Guardian of the Light: Tributes to Archbishop Denis Hurley OMI.* Durban, South Africa: Archdiocese of Durban, 1989.

Ballinger, Margaret. *From Union to Apartheid: A Trek to Isolation.* New York: Praeger Pub., 1969.

Burgess, Julian, Esau duPlessis, et al. *The Great White Hoax: South Africa's International Propaganda Machine.* London, Africa Bureau, 1977.

Cornevin, Marianne. *Apartheid: Power and Historical Falsification.* Paris: UNESCO, 1980.

Davenport, T.R.H. *South Africa: A Modern History.* Toronto: University of Toronto Press, 1977.

De Gruchy, John. *Cry Justice!: Prayers, Meditations and Readings from South Africa.* London: Collins Liturgical Publications, 1986.

Ellis, George. "Lobbying for the Truth." *Sash: Focus on Corruption* (Mowbry, South Africa) 33 (Sept 1989): 5-7.

Omond, Roger. *The Apartheid Handbook: A Guide to South Africa's Everyday Racial Policies.* Middlesex, England: Penguin Books, Ltd., 1985.

PACSA. *Factsheet No. 34: Apartheid's Health System.* Pietermaritzburg, South Africa: Pietermaritzburg Agency for Christian Social Awareness, 1989.

Paton, Alan. *Instrument of Thy Peace.* New York: Seabury Press, 1968.

Sachs, E.S. *The Anatomy of Apartheid.* London: Collet's, 1965.

Terreblanche, Sompi. "The Brotherhood Syndrome: The Origins of Favoritism." *Sash: Focus on Corruption* (Mowbry, South Africa) 33 (Sept 1989): 10-11.

Thompson, Leonard. *The Political Mythology of Apartheid*. New Haven: Yale University Press, 1985.

U.S. Government Foreign Area Studies. *South Africa: A Country Study*. Edited by Harold D. Nelson. Prepared for the Secretary of the Army by the American University. Washington D.C.: Government Printing Office, 1981.

Unrau, Henry. Unpublished report on the South Africa Defense Force raid in Gaborone, Botswana, 1985.

Wallis, Jim and Joyce Hollyday, eds. *Crucible of Fire: The Church Confronts Apartheid*. Maryknoll, New York: Orbis Books, 1989.

Other

Cribbs, Art. "Today's Racist: Liberal, Informed, Experienced and Exposed." United Church Board for World Ministries publication, 1993.

Eliot, T.S. *"Four Quartets." Burnt Norton*. New York: Harcourt, Brace & Company, 1943.

Graves, Robert. *The Greek Myths*. Baltimore, Maryland: Penguin Books, 1955.

McIntosh, Peggy. "White Privilege: Unpacking the Invisible Knapsack." *Peace and Freedom* (July/August 1989): 10-12.

Overeaters Anonymous, *For Today*. Torrance, California: Overeaters Anonymous, Inc., 1982.